It doesn't tell you about all the Tintorettos and Veroneses and Titians you must look at. It just tells you how to enjoy yourself
Ham and High

A world authority on Venice
Jeffrey Bernard *in* The Spectator

J. G. Links' little charmer The Lady

Thanks J. G. Let's do it again
Sue Lawley *in* The Sunday Telegraph

A quite brilliant oddity. Country Living

Funny and fascinating, it is invaluable on the ground but also a beautiful piece of descriptive reading
Eothen

One of the great travel books
The Art Newspaper

My all time favourite guidebook
James Daunt *of* Daunt's Travel Books

The grand old man of Venice
Brian Sewell *in the* Evening Standard

A friend The Daily Mirror

Essential on any Venetian outing
The Sunday Telegraph

Mr. Links leads the visitor on a number of walks through the labyrinthine ways of the most beautiful of cities, walks filled with history, art, observation, curiosities, exotica, and sophistication. It's a guide which like no other I know, leads, by gloriously digressive routes, straight into the heart of a city's genius A Common Reader

A minor classic The Sunday Times

The best guide to Venice The Daily Telegraph

Essential reading Condé Nast Online

Venice with passion The Guardian

J. G. Links' magic guidebook
The Times

One of those miraculous books that gets passed by hand, pressed urgently on friends
Sean French *in the* New Statesman

J.G.Links VENICE

This is the eighth revised edition of a guide book that has become a minor classic, remaining in print for over forty years. Its simple object, in the author's own words, is to guide the reader to places he might otherwise miss and, having reached them, to tell him what he might wish to know and then leave him, preferably at a café, to admire, to enjoy, and perhaps be disappointed. The illustrations show the visitor, as he confronts a view, what his predecessors of a hundred, two hundred or five hundred years ago saw from the same point. Two sections of colour plates have been added, showing how the beauty of Venice inspired the 18th-century view painters.

The main part of the book describes four walks, each of which can be completed in one day, although there are points in each at which one can break off and return another day. Maps, old and new, are provided for each walk. The introduction deals with the Piazza S. Marco and its neighbourhood, and appendices are devoted to the public boat services, food and drink and books about Venice. One chapter is entitled 'Venice for Children's Pleasure'.

FOR PLEASURE

CONTENTS

Foreword

Jan Morris

Innumerable foreigners have been associated with Venice down the generations, but I venture to say that none have been more affectionately related than J. G. Links – on the one side because his was a profound and guileless love of the city, on the other because none of Venice's innumerable chroniclers have portrayed the Serenissima's character with quite such a combination of the scholarly, the informal and the intimate.

I was almost tempted to call his attitude innocent, and in a way it was, because his book is not only called Venice for Pleasure, it really is a sort of pleasure-manual, too. Its author describes himself as 'the perennial tourist', travelling purely for enjoyment, but it would be misleading to think of it as a work of hedonism, for Joe Links was a man of deceptive sophistication, the kind of urbanity that is masked in simplicity. Over the years thousands of readers, starting to reading this book, have been relieved to encounter its famously undemanding approach to the city – 'Generally the first thing to do in Venice is to sit down and have some coffee': but by the time they get to the end of it, all the same, they will have learnt virtually everything that an educated stranger needs to know about the place, its art and its history, besides being subtly entertained throughout.

*   *   *

This has happened almost without their realizing it, for the Links literary style is at once deceptive and essentially *kind*. He is the very opposite of those noisy tour guides we are sure to pass, brandishing their placards, as we follow his easy prose through the streets. He never pushes us, never bullies, never shows off, never condescends. We don't have to be interested in 14th century mosaics, and Venice for Pleasure is surely the only guide-book – if a guide-book is the word for it – that occasionally confesses itself surfeited with wonders, or bored in a gallery of art.

Style, as de Buffon said, is the man himself. I know of no writer whose work seems more organic, as if it has never been worked out in study and draft, but has flowed straight from his mind, like conversation. That mind, though, is marvellously well-stocked. Links' learned devotion to this particular city is supported by astonishingly wide-ranging resources of learning and experience. He was, it is true, one of the world's great authorities on Canaletto, that quintessentially Venetian painter, but as he leads you so engagingly from Rialto to the Piazza, or scoffs at some art historian's unwelcome theory concerning Carpaccio – as he mellifluously rambles on, you would hardly guess that he was also the Queen's Furrier, that he was a familiar competitor on the Cresta Run, that he collaborated on best-selling detective stories, that he wrote a seminal book about urban landscape painting, that he knew a great deal about German wines and was a Governor of the Hudson's Bay Company and loved fast cars and was, altogether, a genuine 20th-century polymath.

'If all the circumstances are propitious,' he says almost at the end of his book, 'I can promise you the most delightful experience that even Venice has to offer.' He is talking about an out-of-season dinner at the Locanda Cipriani on the island of Torcello, and we can sure that his own pleasure is tinged by the memory of some lovely evening of his own, long ago perhaps: but it is enriched too by all the ravishing delights of Venice through which he has been guiding us since the first page – delights sensual very often, but delights of the intellect too, enhanced by humour and by the deep knowledge of history and art that he has been so entertainingly sharing with us.

For by now, as we reach the end of the book, too, we feel we know him well. It has been a walking-tour of Venice, but not exactly a guided tour. He carries no placard, and he has never told us what we ought to do, what we ought to feel. Like an unassuming friend he has shown us the way, helped us to understand, opened our eyes to unexpected beauties and assured us that just to sit at a cafe and look at the passing scene is as essential to the experience of Venice as a visit to the Doge's Palace. His book is properly titled. It really is a handbook to pleasure in Venice.

*   *   *

So far as I know Joe Links, who died in 1997, never complained about what has happened to Venice – its debilitating flooding, its ghastly overcrowding, the vulgarities of its tourist industry and its gradual decline from civic grandeur into the condition of a museum. He loved it, I would assume, for what it was, pathos and all, and like me he relished not only its ancient serenity, but also its gaudy ostentation – which is, after all, as old as the Republic itself.

Anyway, physically little has changed in the city since the first edition of *Venice for Pleasure* was published in 1966 – by the nature of things the structure of Venice remains inviolate, give or take a conversion here, a rebuilding there, or the insidious effects of high water. 'Once again,' Links wrote in the fifth edition, 'I have resisted the temptation to make changes,' and he was right to do so. It is not just that the Venice he takes us through is his Venice, illuminated by his unique personality: it is eternal Venice, Venice in the ideal, almost in the abstract, itself essentially impervious to tourism (if not to tides).

In fact, I think, *Venice for Pleasure* is one of those very few guide-books in the English language which can stand permanently on their own as literature, like Richard Ford's *Handbook to Spain* or E. M. Forster's *Guide to Alexandria*. By the nature of things not much of importance in this book can really be out-dated: but even if, one dread day, the loveliest of all cities is swallowed finally into the Adriatic, a world then bereft can still be lovingly guided around the memory of Venice, stopping for refreshments now and then ('Choose one of the cafes on the Riva del Vin, and settle down. We can now do some sightseeing in comfort') in the incomparable company of Joseph Gluckstein Links.

Trefanmarys, 2008

Preface to the Sixth Edition

No reference has been made to restorations which are taking place throughout Venice and will doubtless continue in the foreseeable future. The reader must not therefore expect to find everything as described in the guide or, in many cases, to be able to see the monument at all. The journey will rarely be wasted, though: a part of Venice that might otherwise have been missed will be seen and the object of this guide is to introduce Venice to its readers rather than her monuments.

The waterbus services will appear very different from those described in earlier editions, apart from the substitution of the name ACTV for the long familiar ACNIL. Within a short period after the publication of this edition they must be expected to change again so that anything said about them here should be checked (except, I feel confident, the venerable No. 1).

Yet again I have resisted the temptation to make changes which a maturer mind would write differently, if at all. Yet again I must rejoice in the miracle that has enabled Venice to survive for thirteen hundred years and this modest guide for over thirty.

This edition is dedicated to Alexander Fyjis-Walker, the perfect publisher – at last.

J. G. Links   London, Autumn 1997

Preface to the Eighth Edition

Though there have indeed been changes in Venice since J. G. Links last wrote, not least to his beloved water-bus services, it is a source of continuous wonder, as he would have put it, that this guidebook can remain essentially unchanged. Forty-two years after its original publication, *Venice for Pleasure* is still adding to the gaiety of nations.

For this edition we are particularly grateful to J. G. Links' grandson Adam Pallant, for so carefully checking all the walks. Revisions have been kept to a minimum so as to preserve the essence of the book as untouched as possible. Change does take place, however, and the reader is advised in particular to consult the vaporetti timetables. There will always be a café table at which such pleasurable work can be undertaken.

Just before his death, J. G. Links was very involved in the restoration of one of the greatest views ever painted of Venice, Canaletto's *The Riva degli Schiavoni* in the Sir John Soane Museum in London. Details have been reproduced in the preceding pages, and it is seen in its entirety opposite

This edition is dedicated to the memory of J. G. Links, the best friend a reader – or publisher – could have.

AFW, London 2008

Venice in 1500. Bird's-eye view by Jacopo de' Barbari. From the wood engraving in the Correr Museum, Venice.

Introduction

I. Author to reader. If I start with the time-honoured words, 'This is not a guide book,' the reader will inevitably expect a series of personal reflections and anecdotes inspired by a stay in Venice, and he would be badly misled. Nor would the denial be quite justified, for this is, in a sense, a guide book. The trouble is that it is only half what a reader expects of a guide book: it is a guide to the pleasures of Venice without its pains. Its simple object is to guide the reader to places he might otherwise miss and, having reached them, to tell him what he might wish to know and then leave him there to admire, to enjoy or, perhaps, to be disappointed.

For let it be said at once, many people are disappointed in Venice. 'Do you know what he said to me when he came back from Venice?' a distinguished old gentleman asked me once; 'he said he was *disappointed*! I must say I envied him his power of imagination.' That seemed to me to sum it up until I cross-examined a very old aunt who also confessed to disappointment with her first visit. In this case the explanation was simple. An exhibition called 'Venice in London' had opened at Olympia in December 1891, and here was Venice as it should have been. It was 'beautifully illuminated and perfectly warmed so that on a winter's day in London a Venetian summer's day could be enjoyed.' The Rialto, the canals, the palaces, the shops, the market places, the very atmosphere and climate were reproduced. There were thousands of lights and dazzling splendour, battalions of graceful and refined danseuses, and lovely Italian music written especially (I am quoting from The Times, so it must be true). On the Canal in front of the stage you could float down the silent waters in a Venetian gondola steered by a Venetian gondolier, accompanied by the music of mandolins and songs of serenaders with their never ending Funiculi-Funicula. AND, The Times fails to point out, although my aunt remembered, the gondolas were WHITE. Later on, in February, she went to Venice, in Italy, for her honeymoon. There were no lights, no warmth, no 'dancers attired in gorgeous costumes' as there had been in London. The canals smelt and, worst of all, the gondolas were black. She returned to Olympia but never to Venice.

But the reader of this guide will probably not be disappointed in Venice. It is, on the whole, not a disappointing city, even to those with enviable powers of imagination. Before forecasting my reader's reactions, though, it might be best to describe him, if only to ensure that those who fail to answer the description refrain from buying this book.

First of all, he is the possessor of at least one other guide to Venice, one that will tell him of the painters and sculptors and architects of Venice and of their marvellous works which fill the treasure houses of the city to overflowing – that is, of course, provided he wants to read about these things as well as to look at them. Be that as it may, this is for the most part a book about the outsides of buildings, seldom about their contents. It is about Venice, the city, not about its possessions, and very little about its people.

Next, he is a walker, or, at least, a dawdler. Earlier writers on Venice seem never to have taken a step through its streets; on arrival they hired a gondola, preferably with two gondoliers, for the period of their stay, and in it they sat, with Ruskin or Baedeker or E. V. Lucas on their lap, occasionally raising their eyes to see what they were gliding past It was a luxurious and enchanting way to see Venice. It still is, in spite of the motor traffic, but you should bear in mind Hugh Honour's warning that in a gondola three is a crowd. This makes it rather expensive.

Nevertheless, contrary to the idea held by

many before their first visit to Venice, there is not a building in the city proper that cannot be reached on foot and the spread of cafés on land has done much to compensate for the loss of amenities on the water. This being the case, it seems only sensible to walk in Venice; nowhere else will the walker be so well rewarded, and the streets, hard though their surfaces appear, have a miraculous spring in the paving which makes fatigue almost impossible.

As to the reader's other attributes, or defects, well, he is not a sightseer in the true sense; he is, for example, prepared to sacrifice the famous and illustrious for the little known and charming if there is not time for both. He is in Venice to enjoy himself, nothing more, and in this, curiously enough, he is in a minority.

Very few travellers seem to enjoy their first visit to Venice. They are awed, dazzled, overwhelmed by its appearance. Its sights arouse their admiration, or, sometimes, their disgust. They marvel at its art, grow incredulous as they learn its history and thank heaven fasting for its existence. Above all, they are exhausted by it; physically, mentally and emotionally, its assault is too much for the ordinary human being to withstand in the few days usually at his disposal. He flees to Florence, where everything has its feet firmly on the ground.

The pure indulgence in pleasure is something denied to all but a handful of travellers willing to devote themselves to seeking nothing else. Their gondola photographs will be inferior to those of their friends; they will know little more of Titian than they knew before leaving home (and much less than if they had stayed at home and read a good book about him); they might not even have entered the Doge's Palace, preferring to leave it until next time, or next time but one. But they will have enjoyed themselves; Venice will have woven its spell around them and they will be captives for life. There will always be time to go into the Doge's Palace later.

It is for them that this book is written.

Now that we know the reader, perhaps we should say something of the writer. Let us exchange references, so to speak. I must start, then, by warning you against me. I am too apt to see Venice through the eyes of John Ruskin because it was he who introduced me to the city through his writings over fifty years ago. Inevitably, therefore, it is the Byzantine traces or the Gothic building that catch my eye and I accept too readily Ruskin's derision of the High Renaissance and of what we now call the Baroque. Yet, with an inconsistency worthy of the great man himself, I am attracted by the painters who chose to explore the visible world rather than by those Ruskin himself admired for their preoccupation with the sublime and the mystical. Giovanni Bellini, Carpaccio or Canaletto will draw me into a church or gallery while Titian, Tintoretto or Tiepolo find me still at my coffee when it is closing time. Nor can I tell you much about the Venetian people for I have never lived among them, preferring the comforts of the Hotel Danieli for short periods two or three times a year over a period of half a lifetime.

Enough of me. It is already apparent that this book is being written by a man with the mind of the perennial tourist. And so it is. My defence is that it is being written *for* the perennial tourist – the tourist, as I see him, being one who travels for pleasure and nothing else whatever. Moreover, the true sightseer is already well served in Venice. He has for long had at his disposal Giulio Lorenzetti's *Venice and its Lagoon* with its 1,000 pages of mostly accurate information, and, since this book was first written, Hugh Honour's *Companion Guide to Venice* has been published. This is the best guide to any city that I happen to have come across, written as it is by a sensitive art historian nevertheless capable of being witty and even descending to gossip.

The plan of this book is simple. It follows the method first laid down by a Major Douglas in 1907 in a now almost unobtainable book called *Venice on Foot* consisting of a series of walks covering most parts of the city. This method was followed by Lorenzetti and Honour but, whereas they take you to places so that you may go inside, Major Douglas and I take you more for the pleasure of the journey. They stop at a church or gallery. We stop at a café – and, in the case of mine, at any rate (there were fewer cafés in Major Douglas's time), are designed to include as many cafés as possible which are suitable resting places where this book may, without self-consciousness, be taken out and read while the objects it describes are ranged around the reader's coffee or apéritif table.

Venice is a city of churches and palaces and, inevitably, since this is both a pleasure guide and a street guide, its emphasis is on palaces rather than churches. A word must be said about Venetian 'streets'. The main streets are, of course, the canals (or *Rii*, singular *Rio*). It was always to the water that the buildings put their best face forward, if there was water to be seen. All secular buildings were approached, by the owners and their guests anyway, from the water. Churches, being patronised more by non-gondola owners, were generally approached by foot. As time has passed, moreover, the demand for foot passage way in certain places became greater than for waterway and many canals were filled in and became dry-land streets. (Where the name is *Rio Terrà* this has invariably occurred.)

A 'street', therefore, may be either a canal or a more conventional roadway (generally *Calle*). (See p. 256 for definitions of all these names.) Very seldom will the front of a palace be on the side away from the water but there is almost always a place from which it can be seen from dry land. One of the objects of this book is to find those places.

II. Approaching Venice. There are many ways of beginning a guide book. You could start with something of the history of the people who inhabit the place. Ruskin (although *The Stones of Venice* is not a guide book and not very much about Venice) did so, and did so in noble words: 'Since the dominion of men was asserted over the ocean, three thrones, of mark beyond all others, have been set upon its sands: the thrones of Tyre, Venice and England.'

The history of the people of Venice is, however, so startlingly unlike that of any other people, and its span so much longer, that to do so would delay the reader's arrival too long. Ruskin's reader, indeed, was delayed by a whole volume and this was because the history led to the architecture and Ruskin felt that to understand the architecture of Venice it was necessary to understand Architecture. This took 140,000 words, most of them well worth reading today, although Venice is scarcely mentioned. Nevertheless, the visitor must know just a little about Venetian history and, as soon as we find somewhere comfortable to sit and spend ten minutes on its study, I propose to provide him with the barest outline of it. He will learn soon enough that this city is unlike any other in the world: a brief look at its history will tell him why.

Another way is to start with a description of the geographical features which made Venice what it is (and what it is gradually becoming). Here again, something of Venice's strange situation in its lagoon, of that eggshell which protects it from the sea and of the reason why its streets are 'full of water' (in Robert Benchley's words) must be known by the traveller who is to enjoy it to the full. The knowledge must wait, though. I must not fall into the trap that ensnared Ruskin. I will start by *going* to Venice and considering the rest when we get there. The air photograph overleaf will give the reader the necessary sense of his bearings.

It has often been said that the only proper way of arriving in Venice is by the sea, that is to say through the northernmost of the two openings in the eggshell to Venice's east (A), and so along the Riva degli Schiavoni (B), perhaps to stop short of everything worth seeing and moor alongside one of the few uninteresting parts of the city (C) (as many of the cruising ships do), or perhaps to continue past all the wonders of the Piazzetta to the Marittima (D), which has nothing to offer but views of dockyards and a brewery.

Those who enter from the airport who do not have a pre-arranged boat to meet them, and cannot afford to hire one, will probably take the Alilaguna service to S. Marco; they will have all the advantages of the arrival by sea but, after what most will find a thrilling voyage, their boat will land them in the heart of the greatest constellation of beauty in all Europe (Plates 1 and 2). It is true that they do not enter the sea itself. Their boat leaves the airport on the main-

land (E), follows a channel in the lagoon to the island of Murano (F) (p. 207), and there enters the main canal of that island. After a stop there it proceeds, passing between the eastern tip of Venice and the island of Certosa, to the Lido for another stop. It continues past the southern bank of Venice, for the most part called the Riva degli Schiavoni, may stop at the Arsenal and so to a mooring point (G) on the Molo, outside the public gardens. We will leave them there to recover their breath until they are rejoined by those who have taken the only slightly more prosaic route from the other direction. They may be interested to know that if they continue on foot for a few yards in the direction their boat was going, they will find themselves outside Harry's Bar. They used to be able, and may one day be able again, to take their first coffee at a delightful little white marble gazebo which was once used as the air terminal and is now the Tourist Information Office. It was built in 1812 and has ever since been a significant little landmark in innumerable drawings, paintings and photographs of the entrance to the Grand Canal, looking west. It was Napoleon who had it built. He liked to take his coffee there and, when told it was a poison, replied that it was a very slow and very delicious one, so we have a good precedent. (It should be noted that most stories told of Napoleon refer in fact to his stepson, Eugène de Beauharnais, who was left as viceroy. There is no evidence that Napoleon himself ever had a day of leisure in Venice.)

Those interested in the strange, malevolent, pathetic work of Fr. Rolfe, Baron Corvo, will be moved to know that they are on the spot where he endured such harrowing and well-deserved suffering.

Most foreign travellers who do not fly into Venice arrive by car or bus (some do so coming from the airport). Probably none come by horse or by carriage, the method used to transport Venice's visitors for the first thousand years of its existence, but quite a number, particularly Italians, continue to use the railway, almost as outdated though it be.

The train traveller has his first glimpse of the lagoon soon after the train leaves Mestre and crosses the two-mile-long bridge begun in 1841. It was built by the Austrians, who were then ruling Venice, but paid for by the Venetians, much to their disgust. They never really wanted a railway bridge and even less did they want a road bridge. They managed to do without the road bridge for another ninety years and had Mussolini on their side – he never believed in the railway bridge either and said he would like to see it pulled down. Before the railway bridge was built, the traveller entered his gondola or the post boat at Mestre or at Fusina, leaving his carriage, if he had one, at the inn before embarking. (It was possible to take one's carriage by boat into the city itself and many did so, although it is hard to see why; when the bridge was finished and the trains started, one often saw carriages hitched on to the back of the train.) Murray's Hand-Book advised travellers to go by way of the village of Fusina rather than the town of Mestre, partly because it had a decent inn where they took care of your carriage and partly because the road to Fusina, by the banks of the Brenta, abounded with neat villas, many of them Palla-

dian (which did not mean that Palladio had built them all). 'The traveller may,' continued Murray, 'if he chooses, proceed by the *barca*, with a very miscellaneous assortment of passengers; and those who do not mind *roughing it* speak of the voyage as affording much pleasure.' We shall later discuss the pleasures of this voyage (see p. 225); meanwhile we are on the railway, which had opened just in time for the 1846 edition of Murray's Hand-Book.

As the train passes over the bridge it is worth casting an eye over the marshes and islands to the north; there is not much to be seen of Venice yet, anyway. This was the scene of the bitter fighting following the rising under Daniele Manin against the Austrians in 1848-49. The bridge had been opened only two years and it became a strategic point in the battles, losing forty of its arches. It was not reopened until 1851. Halfway across there is a monument to the men who rose under Manin against the occupiers. The scene should be borne in mind: moving illustrations of incidents which took place in this neighbourhood will be seen when we visit the Risorgimento section in the Correr Museum later on.

The train arrives at Venice's pride and joy, its new railway station (H), opened in 1955. It replaced the first station for which, in 1846, two churches, two convents, a palace and a scuola were demolished (Plate 29). For over a thousand years the Grand Canal has flowed past this spot.

The traveller by car is in a rather unenviable position. Until 1933 he was not suffered to enter Venice at all with his vehicle. Since then a bridge alongside the railway bridge has admitted him as far as a pair of garages on a site known as the Piazzale Roma. However, these are always full and he may be directed to a vast car park on an adjoining artificial island called the Tronchetto. If this also is full he will have been directed to a car park on the mainland either at S. Giuliano or Fusina whence he will enter Venice by water, as did all his predecessors for a thousand years until 1846. We will assume that he has had the doubtful privilege of parking on the Tronchetto and has thus reached the Piazzale Roma. His dismay may be tempered by the knowledge that he is not yet in Venice at all. The land he stands on and the water beside it were put there for his convenience.

Both the railway traveller and the driver now face the problem of getting themselves, their families and their possessions to their hotel. They (our two travellers) are, moreover, very near each other. The Ferrovia, or railway station, is the water bus's last stop on the Grand Canal proper; the Piazzale Roma is on a modern extension of the Grand Canal and is its final stop. This water bus is the *vaporetto*, the normal means of transport of all Venetians.

A profound knowledge of the internal transport system of Venice may be acquired with comparatively little effort over a number of coffees or aperitifs by means of the ACTV timetable. (This was happily called the ACNIL timetable in earlier editions of this guide and, since the company changed its name to Azienda Consorzio Transporti Veneziano, Venetians still often try to make an acronym of the initials with varying results.) The timetable itself is hard to obtain, but a summary, some may call it a eulogy, will be found in Appendix A. It should be run through at the first convenient opportunity. The effort will be found highly rewarding, but at this point, unless transport has already been arranged, the rich traveller visiting Venice for the first time may indulge in the extravagance of a water taxi. If the weather is fine, and the traveller's anxiety to reach his destination can be contained, the gondola is probably preferable, and, of course, cheaper (but by no means cheap). The porters will require to be tipped according to what will seem an excessive scale, but one which is legally laid down. A small tip will also be required for the man who holds the boat alongside during embarkation. He is called a *ganzier* and is probably a retired gondolier: his predecessors have been tipped for just this service for a great many centuries and it is not for a stranger to break the tradition. (On the whole, there is not a great deal of tipping or alms-giving to be expected in Venice. Beggars are comparatively few, although it is painful to see the occasional child playing happily until he catches sight of a tourist and then adopting an expression of misery to gain sympathy and money. It is true that the visitor cannot be unconscious of the general intention to make him pay to the full for the privilege of being in Venice. The charges are nearly all prescribed by law, though, and the privilege is one worth paying for. Always remember that whatever the Municipality extracts from today's tourists will not be enough to preserve Venice from extinction for much more than another hundred years.)

Many of us will, however, happily turn to the *vaporetto*, and board a No. 1, or possibly, in the summer, the faster Nos. 3 or 82. (ACTV in its wisdom changes its routes from year to year but it is safe to assume that No. 1 is sacrosanct.) As no one in his senses will proceed on the magical journey now about to start with a guide book on his lap, no detailed description of the buildings need be given here. Like all the best journeys, it is not the most direct way to reach our destination. The Grand Canal follows the shape of an inverted letter S and if the top loop were cut off two miles of what would otherwise be a three-mile journey could be avoided. Mussolini made this possible by having a new canal (called, indeed, the Rio Nuovo) cut to join an old canal which enters the Grand Canal at a point near the curve of the bottom loop (thus, for once, reversing the process of closing long-standing canals and replacing them by streets, a process which has done much to upset the precarious balance between water and land and tide on which Venice's existence depends). But the boat that used to take this route, the *diretto*, is no more, and today's traveller will have to imagine the pleasures of sailing past the Venice Fire Station and Venetian traffic lights.

Our destination is the S. Marco stop. We are approaching the Piazzetta down the Grand Canal (K) from the opposite direction to that taken by the travellers who came by the airport boat and whom we now join on the Molo. (In fact, of course, we shall probably first go to our hotel but I omit that part, so anxious are we to join our fellow travellers and get started. In a way this is a pity since the arrival at one's hotel by boat is the first of the many supreme pleasures which Venice, and Venice alone, offers. Its nature varies with each hotel, and some of the smaller ones have, indeed, to be approached on foot just as if one were anywhere else. Most hotels, though, are converted palaces, or at any rate on the sites of palaces, and it is worth remembering that only when we arrive, or leave, by boat shall we in all probability be using the front door. If we happen to be staying at the Danieli, this will no longer be the case, but in Ruskin's day 'the beginning of everything was in seeing the Gondola-beak come actually inside the door at Danieli's, when the tide was up, and the water two feet deep at the foot of the stairs.')

III. View from the Molo. But we are on the Molo and perhaps the first thing to do, as is generally the first thing to do in Venice, is to sit down and have some coffee. Since we cannot take it at 'Napoleon's' coffee house at the old air terminal, we shall have to drink expensively at a table facing the Lagoon which is part of the Piazzetta cafés with a band. (Those arriving from the Grand Canal may not yet have seen the Piazzetta – but be patient.) If we have not yet

bought Italian currency we may have to find a free marble seat and do without coffee.

We look around us. Ahead, and slightly to our left is the church of S. Giorgio Maggiore on its own island. We shall visit it, if only to climb its campanile and see the best view of all of Venice. Palladio designed the church and its adjoining buildings which were not finished until 1614, more than thirty years after his death. To many of us, Palladio's pure lines stand for Renaissance architecture at its noblest, although it is not to Venice but to Vicenza we must go to see his work in its full flower. Ruskin considered S. Giorgio barbarous, childish and contemptible. Palladio's was the infidel art that Ruskin hated. Indeed, Ruskin had chosen Venice because it was 'in Venice only that effectual blows can be struck at this pestilent art of the Renaissance. Destroy its claims to admiration there,' he wrote, 'and it can assert them nowhere else.' For Goethe, on the other hand, Palladio 'opened the way to all art and life as well'. How different was his work from 'our saints, squatting on their stone brackets and piled one above the other in the Gothic style, or our pillars which look like tobacco pipes, our spiky little towers and our cast-iron flowers. Thank God, I am done with all that junk for good and all.' We may choose between them.

Opposite is a drawing showing the scene where we are sitting as it was in Canaletto's day. The little building in the foreground was behind the Tourist Office – in fact it *is* behind, since you can still see the remains of the arch and window if you cross the bridge. It was called the Fondeghetto della Farina, a small wheat warehouse, but later on it had become the headquarters of the Minister of Wheat Supply for the city. The public granaries are on the right of the drawing and they occupied that site until 1808. Soon after that, the gardens were laid out and the little building we are sitting by was built in front of the Fondeghetto della Farina. The Fondeghetto itself, which had by that time become the Academy of Fine Arts, was given to the port authorities and it still houses the Captain of the Port.

We have now met both Ruskin and Canaletto and their names will appear often in this book.

25

This is simply because they, more perhaps than any other two people, left a record of what Venice looked like in their day, Ruskin in words (but in a good many accomplished drawings, too), Canaletto in pictures. Canaletto's day was, moreover, a very beautiful one for Venice and his superb records of it are readily available in the Wallace Collection, the National Gallery, Woburn Abbey, Windsor Castle and in many, perhaps too many, reproductions. And he was a marvellous painter and the modern tendency to decry him as a mere topographer, or a mere anything else, must be put down with firmness. It is true that he became mechanical when the pressure on him to produce more and more pictures became too heavy; he ended by producing a succession of scratches and blobs (some say he was never the same after he returned to Venice from England, but he had deteriorated before he went to England). Fortunately, we have in the National Gallery what are probably his two best pictures, *The Stonemason's Yard* and *The Scuola S. Rocco* (as is the case with so many painters represented in the National Gallery by

their best work). *The Stonemason's Yard* (it is reproduced on p. 75 and we shall be going to the spot where it was painted) even converted Ruskin who had written a great deal of nonsense about Canaletto in his youth. When he saw it with the *Scuola S. Rocco* for the first time in the National Gallery he said, 'I may as well make a clean breast of it; I even found myself admiring Canaletto's pictures of Venice.' This was fairly generous in view of what he had himself described as his 'determined depreciation' of Canaletto's work but he had in fact seen extremely few Canaletto pictures and there is no evidence that he had *ever* seen a good one until that moment.

As for Ruskin's day in Venice, well perhaps it was a little dingy under the Austrian rule with most of the buildings sadly decaying – although there was plenty of social life, as we know from reading the letters of his wife, Effie. Ruskin though, made everything he touched magical, either with his words or his drawings, and there could be no more entertaining companion through the Streets of Venice. We can enjoy his opinions without taking them too seriously and his facts are nearly always unassailable – well nearly, nearly always.

But we are looking at S. Giorgio Maggiore with our own eyes, by the grace of God, not Ruskin's or Canaletto's. Good or bad architecture, there can hardly be another church in such a position or one so often painted and photographed. The steeple of the campanile was not built until 1791, after another had fallen down in the way campaniles have. Its sides are straight, as were those of S. Giorgio's first campanile. Between 1728 and 1774, though, the steeple had onion-shaped sides, a useful thing to remember when looking at Canaletto's many pictures of this scene as it sometimes enables one to recognise a pre-1728 picture.

On the right of the island of S. Giorgio, as we are looking out on to it, is a narrow strip of water dividing it from the Giudecca, a long, narrow and not very interesting island, separated from the city by a canal also called the Giudecca. Until the Hotel Cipriani was opened in 1958 the island was seldom visited by travellers to Venice except to see another Palladian church called the Redentore (Plate 16) or, perhaps, one of the privately owned villas and gardens on the island.

To our right is the entrance to the Grand Canal, dominated by the church of S. Maria della Salute, painted and photographed as often as S. Giorgio Maggiore itself. To the left of the Salute are the Dogana di Mare (the Custom House), and the Seminario Patriarcale and, at the tip of the land, the little tower with its two Atlases holding up a ball with Fortune on top. It is hard to imagine the Grand Canal without the Salute but, in fact, it was not built until the seventeenth century and not finished until 1687, long after Venice's great days. Before then, the entrance to the Grand Canal gave no indication of the wonders to come as may be seen from Jacopo de Barbari's bird's-eye view of Venice in 1500 – which, it happens, is hanging on a wall scarcely a hundred yards behind our backs awaiting our visit to the Correr Museum. I shall often refer to it and you will find a reproduction of the whole view in the plate on pages 10-11, and a

AEQVORA TVENS
PORTV·RESIDEO
HIC NECTVNVS

PA LA

number of details from it throughout the book, The detail opposite shows the area in which we are now, the Molo (before the Fondeghetto della Farina was built), the Piazzetta and the Piazza, and that on p. 93 shows the area to the west of us, the entrance to the Grand Canal, the Custom House and the palaces which precede what are now the great hotels, several of them still recognisable. You will, I think, often be referring to these details, especially the first.

We can see little enough of our own side of the Grand Canal, but the *vaporetto* station on our right is the S. Marco station, naturally one of the busiest, and it is a little surprising that our own parents would not have been able to reach it from where we are sitting as the little bridge had not been built. The Venetians were less concerned with convenience than with the building of beautiful status symbols.

We finish our coffee and walk eastwards along the Molo. As I have already said, granaries once occupied the area where the gardens now are. Before that, there were boat-building yards (*squeri*; every now and then on our walks we will come across a *squero*, generally of ancient lineage) and a fish market. Before that there was a wall to protect the city from its enemies arriving by sea and this wall continued some distance up the Grand Canal. Before that – but we are already back to the ninth century although Venice had then been a city for some four hundred years.

It was Napoleon who had the granaries pulled down and gardens laid out in their place. The buildings we see behind the gardens are the backs of those forming the south side of the Piazza S. Marco, the whole of which he converted into the Royal Palace. The gardens are full of shady trees, which perhaps seem a little out of place in Venice, but which provide delightful sitting out places. We should certainly, too, enter them and examine the ironwork of the gates and of the canopy over the water entrance to the palace; we can picture the distinguished visitors' gondolas passing under the drawbridge of the little canal leading from the Basin of St. Mark and drawing up at this entrance for them to disembark. After Napoleon, the Palace was occupied by the Austrian governors of the city and then it became the property of the new King of Italy. It so remained until his successors found their palaces too numerous to keep up and Victor Emanuel III generously transferred the burden to the City of Venice after the First World War.

We pass a little club house, this time the Sailing Club, and then the Zecca (Mint), where gold ducats, or *zecchini*, were minted up to 1870. It is now the home of the Marciana Library (lest you ask who Marciana was, it is the adjectival form of St. Mark). We are on Venice's threshold; a few more steps and the front door has been opened. We are in the Piazzetta. We find another table, perhaps simply moving from the Lagoon side to the Piazzetta side of the café we have just left. Let us choose a table close to the monstrous caryatids whose task it is to hold up the portals of the Marciana Library lest they collapse with all the weight of scholarship above them.

IV. The Doge's Palace and the Basilica.

Where we are sitting (Plates 3 and 4) was once a harbour and the water came in as far as the base of the Campanile, which we can see on our left. It cannot be long, in terms of a city of Venice's age before the water returns, and we are enjoying a privilege which, the experts tell us, may well be denied to our grandchildren and certainly to theirs. Already the duckboards which enable one to walk across the flooded Piazzetta, and which have until recently appeared only on days of exceptionally high tides, are now left out for the whole winter. Venice is sinking (or the waters rising, according to the way you look at it) at the rate of a foot every hundred years and the efforts needed to stop its doing so would daunt the confidence of all but the most courageous. But Venice still stands today and is there for us to revel in.

The two great granite columns came from the East, as did so much in Venice, and have been there for nine hundred years. One of them bears the Lion of St. Mark, or what was left of the beast when he came back from France in 1815 after eighteen years there in the company of much other loot. He would probably have needed restoring, anyway, even had he missed his adventure. His companion on the other column is S. Todaro (St. Theodore), Venice's patron saint until his displacement by St. Mark. The guide books say he was a Greek saint but are curiously vague about him. The English traveller Thomas Coryat, who was in Venice in 1612, has a much more likely story – that he was a Venetian General who won so many battles for them that they canonised him. This sounds very Venetian, as does his displacement when he lost his popularity – could he have stopped winning battles? Anyway, he is more likely to have been a General than an Admiral for he has his back turned to the sea. Whoever he was, though, St. Theodore remained undisturbed on his column but slowly disintegrating. Finally, he had to be replaced by the modern copy we now see.

It must have been a difficult business indeed to unload these columns from the ships bringing them from the East and to erect them in the Piazzetta. One of them was lost in the process and, again according to Coryat, 'is yet to be felt within some ten paces from the shore'. The engineer who succeeded in the task was given the gambling monopoly of Venice as a reward but the sessions had to be held between the columns and it was unfortunate that the scaffold for executions stood in the same place. Today, the Municipality keeps the gambling monopoly to itself and conducts its sessions on the Lido in the summer and in a palace far up the Grand Canal (the Vendramin Calergi) in the winter.

Facing us is the Doge's Palace. These are simple words but the emotions aroused are far from simple. Very few people find themselves facing the Doge's Palace without a preconceived picture in their minds of what the experience will have in store for them. Artists and photographers will have done their utmost to rob the scene of its mystery and unexpectedness. But they have never succeeded. How did it achieve that miraculous colour? Why have the columns no bases? How can a building which disregards all the rules be so beautiful? Or is it beautiful? The questions flood the mind but the senses can still perceive.

A Byzantine palace was begun on this site in the ninth century and finished in the twelfth. In the thirteenth, it was left alone, but at the beginning of the fourteenth century the Gothic palace we see now was begun – not the side we are looking at, but the side facing the lagoon and at the end furthest away from us. We had better leave our coffee for a moment and stroll over to look at that façade (Plates 1 and 2).

Two of the windows are lower than the others and this is where the Gothic palace was started. Soon afterwards it was decided to extend it by demolishing the Byzantine palace and carrying the façade all the way along to the Piazzetta corner and round it as far as the seventh column. This was in order to provide a Council Chamber for the Senate with a ceiling painted by Venice's best masters. To see the ceiling paintings, the windows had to be as high as possible, considerably higher than the two existing windows. This would have raised a pretty problem for the Renaissance (or modern) architect, but the old Venetian 'unhesitatingly raised the large windows to their proper position with reference to the interior of the chamber, and suffered the external appearance to take care of

itself. And I believe,' added Ruskin, for the words are his, 'the whole pile rather gains than loses in effect by the variation thus obtained in the spaces of wall above and below the windows.'

This Gothic palace was finished by the beginning of the fifteenth century when the main balcony on the lagoon side was built. The remains of the Byzantine palace adjoined it and by this time the Senate felt that enough money had been spent to impress the most exacting visitor. Fearful that the expansionists would soon want to pull down what was left of the Byzantine palace, they therefore decreed that anyone who even made such a suggestion should be fined a thousand ducats. A fire in 1419 made the Doge of the day, who had to live in the old palace, so uncomfortable that he had the thousand ducats carried into the Council Chamber and begged that the unspeakable should be spoken of. No one opposed him and the thousand ducats were devoted to the expenses of the work. A new Renaissance palace was built on the Piazzetta side – and we can return to our coffee and look at it.

It starts at the seventh column from the sea

(which you will notice is much thicker than the others and has a carving of 'Venice' in the shape of justice above it) and, as will be seen, is just a copy of the Gothic palace – except that the windows are symmetrical; there was no need for the four new windows to be higher than the other two. By 1439 it was finished and forty years later there was a disastrous fire which resulted in some of the best Renaissance architects being called in to reconstruct much of the original work. When we come to enter the courtyard we shall see this work, such as the Giants' Staircase, and when we stand on the Bridge of Straw to photograph the Bridge of Sighs which joins the Doge's Palace to the Prison building to the east of it, we shall see the Renaissance façade of the palace overlooking its narrow canal. Much of this high Renaissance work was being completed while the English were building the Gothic Henry VII's chapel of Westminster Abbey. A Milanese pilgrim, Canon Pietro Casola, was in Venice at the time and wrote bitterly about the Venetians' parsimony in rejecting a scheme to extend the Palace over the small canal by its side. This would have given the Doge a large garden but, he wrote, 'they have not wanted to spend enough'. The site, instead, was occupied by mean buildings until a few years ago when the Hotel Danieli extension was built on it.

Another terrific fire burst out in 1574 leaving most of the building a mere shell. There was talk of throwing down the ruined building and putting up a new one, an idea which Palladio, not unnaturally, supported. What would Venice have looked like with a Palladian palace on this site? The idea is an intriguing one but on the whole it is probably fortunate that the majority of Venetian architects were for restoration. And so it happened.

It was on the capitals of the columns of the lower façade of the palace that the Gothic craftsmen lavished their finest work (the capitals of the Renaissance side, like the façade itself, are mostly copies of those on the lagoon side). All are now restored or replaced by nineteenth-century copies and, indeed, on the side facing the lagoon, some of the columns themselves have been moved nearly a foot in the course of strengthening the building in the 1880's. Even so, they are worth looking at, although not, perhaps, with *The Stones of Venice* in one's hands as the nineteenth-century traveller found essential – seventy pages were devoted to the description of these capitals. Above the capitals there are, at each of the three corners of the palace, figure sculptures with which we shall become increasingly familiar as we pass beneath them. The two facing the lagoon are fourteenth-century, or Gothic, work and the one on the St. Mark's corner, the Judgment of Solomon, is fifteenth-century, that is to say early Renaissance. The one nearest us, on the Piazzetta corner, is the Fall of Man, called by Ruskin the Fig-tree Angle, and the further one, beside the Bridge of Sighs, is the Drunkenness of Noah, which he called the Vine Angle. He attached great weight to the fact that the Gothic sculptors chose to depict human frailty and the Renaissance sculptor preferred human sagacity. He thought it demonstrated the difference in spirit between the two epochs – and perhaps he was right. Above these figures are the three Archangels, Gabriel (in the Piazzetta corner),

Michael and Raphael above the drunken Noah. We need not study every capital or bother ourselves too much about their symbolism. Some are certainly worth examination, though, such as that above the seventh column from the Piazzetta corner, the one which is thicker than all the others. It tells a moving story of a young couple, starting with a lover seeing his mistress at a window, then courting her, bringing her presents, their first kiss, their wedding, the birth and then the childhood of their son and finally the child's death. In Ruskin's day, this column was railed off to protect two guns set there by the Austrian occupiers but, although he admitted not being able to see the sculptures properly, he thought them inferior in design to most others. He preferred the Eight Ages of Man above the next column but one to it (towards the lagoon) or the Tradesmen above the next column to that.

Why no bases? 'The gigantic columns of the portico stand without pedestals all sunk in about forty centimetres underneath the present-day pavement,' says Lorenzetti, the authoritative guide to present-day Venice. 'They were meant to be walked beside without stumbling,' is Ruskin's rather surprising explanation. Yet I have heard modern engineers say that there *were* bases but that the periodic raising of the pavement has concealed them. We shall soon be looking at a picture which includes a corner of the palace in great detail. It was painted when the columns were less than sixty years old and they have no bases. I think this settles the matter conclusively.

It is no use complaining that the Doge's Palace we are looking at is not exactly the same one as Ruskin or Turner or Canaletto or Tiepolo saw. A large part of it is, and we are fortunate to see that part. We can also, if we wish, walk under the arcade all the way along the lagoon side until we come to the canal which leads under the Bridge of Sighs and that is more than any of them could have done. After the 1574 fire the arches at the eastern end of the palace were blocked up to save the building from falling down. They remained so for the next three hundred years as every picture of them shows (and there were many, many pictures of the scene painted in the following three hundred years). It was not until 1889 that they were opened up again – after twenty years of restoration work on the Palace which included removing *every* column of both galleries and replacing or repairing it. What does it matter if St. Theodore or twelve of the thirty-six capitals of the columns were made in a modern workshop principally concerned with funerary memorials? But for such men Venice would have been under the sea a hundred years earlier than it will be now.

Enjoy this miraculous building while you can and defer entering it for as long as possible (perhaps, even, until your next visit). When the time does come, the best, although the most expensive, way of 'doing' it is to hire a portable telephone guide from a girl who will be found hovering around the entrance. She will sling a tape recorder over your shoulder, attach an earphone to your head (and to your companion's, if you have one) and send you off to the sound of cymbals and the cries of medieval Venetian citizens (shouting in English). An invisible radio announcer will now be your companion, telling you when to sit down and which way to turn, warning you to mind the step and providing occasional bursts of music. When you reach the spot where reluctant witnesses were taken away to be tortured, their cries will curdle your blood. After half an hour, intimacy will have developed to such an extent that it will come as no surprise at all when your companion says 'as we enter the next room our representative will be waiting to change the tape' and, lo and behold, a small boy stops sucking his ice cream, rises from his seat and, after some expert work on the inside of the tape recorder, re-garlands you and sends you on your way for another half-hour. On the other hand you will find all the information you are likely to require in the rooms themselves, often enlivened by reproductions of old prints showing the rooms as they were when occupied by real people, not just us tourists.

The main entrance to the Palace courtyard is beneath the Porta della Carta, recently saved from disintegration by the British 'Venice in Peril' fund and preserved indefinitely by the most modern conservation methods. Built in the 1440's, this was almost the last truly Gothic monument to be raised in Venice. To Ruskin it was not Gothic at all: the corruption of the Renaissance had already penetrated and in the Porta della Carta 'vice reached its climax'. Judge for yourself when the time comes.

On the other side of the Porta della Carta is, of course, St. Mark's, begun nine hundred years ago, but remaining merely the Doge's chapel until, in 1807, Napoleon applied French logic and made it the cathedral church of Venice – a status previously held by the church of S. Pietro in the extreme east of the city. The Venetians treated this little façade of St. Mark's rather as their mantelpiece, dotting souvenirs of their travels (for which they had not paid even the sou) here and there. The plain multi-coloured marble annexe to St. Mark's is the Treasury, originally one of the corner towers of the first Doge's Palace. The four clasped figures on the porphyry relief let into its wall came, we are always told, from Acre; so did the two square columns. Some of us may have forgotten that Acre, now in Israel, is a three-thousand-year-old port which achieved a little fame in the Crusades and a very little more when Napoleon was in Egypt. The Venetians took it in 1256 and ever since it seems enough to say that something 'came from Acre' to explain all.

The guide books nowadays say the four clasped figures are Tetrarchs who reigned with Diocletian. Coryat as usual had a better story than the guide books, though, and, according to him they were four brothers who came to Venice on business from Albania with a richly laden shipload of goods. Two of them went ashore, leaving the other two on board, and came to the conclusion that the family fortune was better divided between two brothers than four. They therefore bought some poison for use at dinner that night when the brothers would be reunited. Curiously enough, exactly the same idea had occurred to the brothers remaining on board and they also arrived at dinner equipped with poison. Both drugs worked successfully; all four died and the Venetians seized their goods. As this was Venice's

first windfall, she erected the porphyry memorial to the brothers, quaintly described as 'consulting' together. It seems odd that such a splendid story as this should have been displaced by such a dull one as that of the four Tetrarchs.

The dumpy porphyry pillar at the corner of St. Mark's (it also 'came from Acre') is called the Pietra del Bando. New laws were proclaimed from it, first in Acre, then, since 1256, in Venice. It also had a more macabre use. The heads of traitors to the state were laid upon it after their execution and left there until the smell became too much for the citizens to bear – generally a matter of three or four days. Canaletto painted the Pietra del Bando often, and from it even more often. But with all the venerable years it carried and all the history it must have seen passing by, it was not until 14 July 1902 that it underwent its strangest experience.

At 9.52 a.m. on that day, the Campanile, or bell-tower, which had stood where it now stands for just on a thousand years, decided that that was enough and subsided gently to the ground. No dancer could have fallen more gracefully, if she had to fall. Hardly any damage was done; no one was hurt. The Pietra del Bando was pushed gently on to its side between two of the columns of St. Mark's. Only the Loggetta, the little folly at the foot of the Campanile, was damaged, and this, like the Campanile, became part of a castle of dust. It was not a very high castle: the top barely reached above the upper arcade of the Palace. Its base surrounded the nearest of the three flagpoles outside St. Mark's but only just reached the middle one and damaged neither (there is a photograph of the scene opposite). Probably the whole city knew what was about to happen. Certainly one photographer did; he took up his position on the roof of the Clock Tower and opened his lens just as the gap opened up in the centre of the Campanile. He thus produced a perfect record of what was truly one of Venice's most sensational events and his photograph is on p. 40. A few, but not many, people are seen running away from the falling building. The whole scene appears to be managed with the quiet efficiency of a traditional Venetian intrigue.

Then came the great debate. Should it be rebuilt and, if so, how? Many thought the Piazza looked better without it and there is much to be said for this view. We shall be able to decide for ourselves in due course. The prospect of designing a modern replacement was too daunting (perhaps fortunately: 1902 was not the best period of architectural design anywhere in Europe). The Venetians were used to copying their worn-out buildings. They copied the Campanile. Every detail was reproduced and by 1912 anyone with poor enough eyesight would scarcely have known that anything had happened. In the case of the Loggetta, the pieces of stone were sorted out of the dust of the Campanile and put together again like those of a jigsaw puzzle. In the following sixty years it decayed more than in the previous 362 and was recently saved from disintegration, again by the British 'Venice in Peril' fund. This Loggetta had been built in 1540 by Sansovino who also designed the Library behind us. The Loggetta was originally used as an exclusive club and then as a sort of guard room. It is now used as the entrance to the Campanile and we shall buy

our tickets there. The Library proved a source of much anxiety to its designer, Sansovino. When he arrived in Venice as a refugee from Rome, he found inns, butchers' stalls and wooden public lavatories in the Piazzetta. He also found himself very quickly made chief architect of Venice, a little surprisingly as he had no great reputation either in Florence, his birthplace, or Rome where he worked. He had the inns and lavatories cleared away and set about putting up a group of Roman buildings right opposite the Doge's Palace and St. Mark's. The Library was by far the most important (and the most successful) but, after ten years work, part of it fell down and Sansovino spent a short time in prison as a warning to be more careful in future. Twenty-five years later Sansovino died and it was still unfinished. Scamozzi was then called in and finished the building by 1582.

Baedeker, who influenced Victorian taste more than is generally realised, called the Library one of the finest secular edifices in Italy. This was in 1882 and even by 1913 he had qualified his opinion only to the extent of calling it '*perhaps* the most magnificent secular edifice in Italy'. Presumably he had his back turned to the Doge's Palace when he wrote this and it is time we turned our heads back in that direction. It is time, too, that we paid our bill and returned to our hotel. If we did steal that glimpse of the Piazza we know what is in store for us.

V. St. Mark's: The Piazza. Our first task on returning to the Piazza is to decide whether to patronize Florian's café on the south side or Quadri's on the north. If it is morning and we want shade, it will have to be Florian's and perhaps this is the best choice anyway. It is by far the older of the two, having opened in 1720 and, until fairly recently, boasted that it never closed, day or night. Throughout the Austrian rule, too, it was Florian's which was favoured by the Italians, Quadri's being left for the Austrians: let us not be thought to be invaders.

Once settled at our table, we may look around. Behind us is, or, to be accurate, are the Procuratie Nuove, the new residences of the nine Procurators of Venice, formerly the city's high-est officials. We may remember that Scamozzi was called in after Sansovino's death to finish his Library and he paid Sansovino the compliment of continuing his design for ten arches round the south side of the Piazza. He thought a two storey building would be too low, though, for so large a square, so he added a storey and left it at that.

This was in 1586 and the work then hung fire for a long time. In Coryat's time, 1612, it was 'but little more than half ended', only twenty windows being in place, but he foresaw that when finished it would 'excell the North side in beauty', and in 1640 a new architect, Baldassarre Longhena, was called in to complete the build-ing. He continued it as far as the end, on our left, and then left the top storey off, reverting to Sansovino's original design completely. He had only about a third of the west end of the Piazza to deal with, as a church stood in the middle called S. Geminiano and, on the other side of the church, the Procuratie Vecchie started and these continued round the opposite side of the Piazza, just as they do now. The Procuratie Vecchie were the Procurators' old residences and were begun just a hundred years before the new ones, in 1480. (You can see S. Geminiano as it was in Canaletto's time opposite and, more than two hundred years earlier, in the detail from the Barbari drawing on p. 28. In Barbari's time there was only one upper storey to the Procuratie Vecchie, the second being added in 1512.)

The upper floors of the Procuratie Vecchie have now become the offices of an insurance company whereas the upper floors of our side of the Piazza house the Correr Museum. The insurance company is called the Assicurazioni Generali and they used to express in a practical way their appreciation of occupying what is surely the most privileged office site in the world. Each morning they fed the pigeons, distributing the feed in the shape of a gigantic **AG** on the Piazza pavement so that a tightly wedged pack of pigeons heralded the name of their benefactor until the last grain of corn was eaten. You will sometimes see an old postcard celebrating the one occasion when COCA COLA was emblazoned across the Piazza in exactly the same way, a helicopter being conveniently in the air to record the scene for posterity. Much loved as the pigeons are, by both Venetians and tourists, their unfortunate disregard for sanitation is now recognized as a major cause of stone pollution and they are tolerated rather than encouraged. Rumour has it that attacks are even sometimes made on their fertility by the introduction of a pill to their feed.

Napoleon had the church of S. Geminiano demolished, together with a hundred and sixty-five others. He had no more fear of the Pope than of anyone else or he would have hesitated, for in 1173 the Venetians were put under interdict just for altering the old church when they enlarged the Piazza. The Sansovino-Scamozzi Library design was then carried all the way round the west end of the Piazza and a frieze put on the top of it. You can just see where the new building starts at the seventh arch from our side. You can also see the statues of Roman emperors which adorn it but you will notice a curious blank in the centre. The space was reserved for Napoleon himself but no one has troubled to fill it.

Before 1582, our side of the Piazza was sixty

feet nearer the centre and ended up against the north side of the Campanile, closing it in. If you look at Gentile Bellini's picture of the Piazza in 1496 (opposite) you will see how it then appeared; the building at the end, up against the Campanile, was a hospital.

Gentile Bellini intended you to think that this was the view from the middle of the Piazza but if you stand there you will see that this is not so. St. Mark's does not face towards the middle of the Piazza and from that point the Campanile dominates the scene and masks the Porta della Carta. To get a symmetrical view of St. Mark's, and at the same time push the Campanile into a less obtrusive position, the artist had to move to the north side of the Piazza from where everything fell into place. Since this was no position to watch a procession from he then made it look as if the observer was standing in front of S. Geminiano.

Two hundred and fifty years later Canaletto followed Gentile Bellini's example and never hesitated to move the monuments of Venice like a scene-shifter to achieve the effect he wanted;

all that was necessary was to adopt two or even more viewpoints for the same picture. You may find it an entertaining occupation to identify some of those viewpoints with a reproduction in front of you.

When the arguments about rebuilding the Campanile were raging, the opponents to the idea claimed, rightly, that it had never been intended to be free-standing as it is now and as it has been since Scamozzi's day; its design, they said, was quite unsuitable for such a position and the Piazza was much better without it altogether. It was true, as a Mr Clark wrote to *The Times* in 1903, that for the first time the spectator could now have a clear view from an adequate distance of the 'whole of S. Marco's marvellous façade, of the connecting Porta della Carta and of the exquisite diaper of the Palace.' 'I shall be glad for the rest of my life,' he went on, 'to have had the opportunity of seeing these things even if the opportunity is taken away.' Nobody listened to Mr Clark and within nine years the Campanile had been replaced. Fortunately, photography provides a compensation to the reader who has

been denied the opportunity of seeing these things (until the new Campanile falls down?) and I reproduce the scene just as Mr Clark saw it for those few short months. (See opposite.)

All that is left to us is the little vista between the Campanile and the Procuratie Nuove and we cannot even see the newly restored Porta della Carta. Mr Clark, though (and now, thanks to photography, you and I), could even see through it to the Giants' Staircase in the Courtyard (Plate 6). (It was at the head of these stairs that the Doge stood to be crowned with the little bonnet called *Zoia* which we know from many portraits such as Giovanni Bellini's Doge Leonardo Loredan in the National Gallery, London.)

There is no exit from the Piazza on the side we are sitting. Napoleon converted the whole of this side and the end where S. Geminiano had been, known since as the Ala Napoleonica, Napoleonic wing, into the Royal Palace. A passage by the side of Florian's leads only to the courtyard and excessively steep staircases up to what are now the offices of the Correr Museum. There are two passages under the Ala Napoleon-

ica. The one in the centre was the entrance to the Royal Palace and is now the entrance to the Correr Museum; a staircase leads up to it from the right of the passage. The one nearer us is called the Bocca di Piazza (mouth of the Piazza) and it was the scene from here that Ruskin described in his over-quoted but unforgettable passage beginning, 'for between those pillars there opens a great light, and, in the midst of it, as we advance slowly, the vast tower of St. Mark seems to lift itself visibly forth from the level field of chequered stones . . .' *Stones of Venice*, Vol. 2, Chap. 4 (Plate 7). We shall pass through this passage often, if we have not already done so. It leads to the backs of the great hotels and to the Accademia Bridge, the first point at which we can cross the Grand Canal on foot.

There are six passages leading out of the side facing us, the Procuratie Vecchie. Starting at the Napoleon end, the first leads to the Bacino Orseolo, a great place for gondolas to congregate and so to the S. Luca district, passing the Cavaletto Hotel: it was so named in the fourteenth century when even Venetians travelled on horseback. The next is less frequented but worth exploring. It leads to the Campo S. Gallo, once a fashionable quarter but now rather seedy. The third leads only to a courtyard. The fourth leads to some ancient and fascinating *calli* and buildings. The fifth is another courtyard, and the sixth is under the Clock Tower and leads by way of the Mercerie (literally haberdashers' shops), the principal shopping street of the City, to the Rialto Bridge – and, indeed, to all Venice except the extreme south-eastern and south-western parts. In other words we shall use the Piazzetta and the Riva degli Schiavoni to get to the Arsenal (or the Biennale, if it is on); we shall go through the Bocca di Piazza when we go to the Accademia or explore the Zattere area; we shall use the first passage opposite us, starting at the Bacino Orseolo, when examining the tongue of land bounded by the Grand Canal which includes the S. Luca, S. Angelo, and S. Stefano districts, the Fenice Theatre and many of the most rewarding views from bridges in all Venice. Otherwise, we shall find ourselves always starting with the Mercerie. We shall get to know that

Clock Tower very well, often happening to pass by on the hour when the two Moors gently strike their bell and, if it happens to be Ascension week, we shall see every hour a procession consisting of an angel-herald and the three Magi encircling the Madonna in homage.

At this point, the Piazza proper ends and the Piazzetta dei Leoncini begins. In Canaletto's pictures it is called the Campo S. Basso, but the church of S. Basso was closed a hundred and fifty years ago and the little campo is now called after the two red marble lions put there in 1722, with their backs now worn smooth by the seats of little children. A photograph of the red lions without a child astride them would be as rare a memento of Venice as one of the Piazza without the pigeons being fed. If you turn left off the Piazzetta dei Leoncini you will pass through some good shopping streets before joining up with the Mercerie. If you continue straight across it, you will cross the canal bounding the Doge's Palace *behind* the Bridge of Sighs and find yourself well set for an expedition to the S. Maria Formosa district, SS. Giovanni e Paolo, one of the two great Gothic churches (the other is the Frari on the eastern side) or the Fondamente Nuove, whence you embark for Torcello. All these areas can be reached equally well by going up the Mercerie and turning right off the Campo S. Bartolomeo as soon as the Rialto Bridge comes into sight. Every point in Venice must, however, be approached from at least two different directions if its full pleasure is to be enjoyed. How else would one know which route had the best cafés on it?

All this naming of unknown districts and churches may have confused the newly arrived visitor at his table at Florian's, but it may also have given him a general picture of what lies ahead. None of them need be remembered; they will all be encountered in due course. Meanwhile, there is an object at the end of the Piazza which has not been mentioned. It is St. Mark's.

You may see St. Mark's as a lovely dream, a sea-borne vase of alabaster, the most magical and most mysterious of churches (as Ruskin did at various times) or you may see only 'its ill-shaped domes; its walls of brick encrusted with marble; its chaotic disregard of symmetry; its confused hodgepodge...' and so on which was the characteristic Victorian attitude to it before Ruskin came along. You might even see it as a robber's den and this would be a fairly accurate view, for almost everything in it was stolen. It is unlikely that you will find it a boring building and as it will no doubt be seen very often, and as it will be found difficult to pass any part of it without pausing to examine one of its details, no great attention need be paid to it at the moment. The mosaic in the great lunette over the extreme left-hand door as you look at the church should be observed, though. It is the only one left of the original Byzantine mosaics over the doors of the façade, the others having been done at various times from 1660 to 1836. It shows what St. Mark's looked like before the Gothic additions were made, the 'range of glittering pinnacles', before it was possible for 'the crests of the arches to break into a marble foam and toss themselves far into the blue sky in flashes and wreaths of sculptured spray'. When we go to the Accademia, we shall see the portrayal by Gentile Bellini of

the Piazza as it was in 1496 (reproduced on p. 44). It shows this mosaic, and the others which were still there and which were already old, painted in meticulous detail. Just as the mosaic was old when Bellini painted it in 1496, so the church was old when this mosaic was set above its door – the 'shafts and stones were set on their foundations here while Harold the Saxon stood before the grave of the Confessor' in the first Westminster Abbey of which only a single arch remains standing, Ruskin was fond of reminding us.

Above the main door are the four bronze horses, and few horses indeed can have seen as much of the world. They started perhaps in Greece and were certainly in Rome on Trajan's Arch. From there they found their way to Constantinople and provided part of the loot the Venetians shared with the Crusaders after the sack of that city during the Fourth Crusade, the blackest moment even in Venice's history. First they were put outside the Arsenal, then where they are now, and there they remained until Napoleon appeared and stole from the Venetians much that they had stolen from others, including the four horses. He mounted them in the Place du Carrousel (and we see their arrival there on this print) and they did not get back to St. Mark's for thirteen years when the Austrians restored them. During the First World War they were taken to Rome and again we have an illustration showing them being admired in their new surroundings in the garden of the Palazzo Venezia. Now they are safely inside St Mark's and those you see on the pedestals outside are copies. While their future was being decided one of them was sent on a tour and I found myself beside it in the Royal Academy, London. It was a moving – and surprising – experience and I was not alone in finding it difficult to keep the tears back.

For the first few hundred years of St. Mark's existence, it was reached by ascending steps from the Piazza. Since then, the level of the Piazza has been raised several times and today we step down to enter it. Not only that; the pavement of the Piazza curves down towards it, so that part of the façade may not be actually hidden.

Originally, the Piazza had grass and trees growing in it, and, indeed, was called 'Brolo', or garden. It was doubled in size in the twelfth century and had a colonnade round it, and in 1264 had its first paving of tiles. A hundred

years later, it had to be raised and repaved and two hundred years after that the process had to be repeated. There were still trees and vines in it, though, and it was not until 1722 that the first stone pavement was laid. Three of Canaletto's earliest Piazza paintings tell us what it looked like then but in all the others the paving is exactly as we see it today. Before and after the repaving, there were always canvas booths depicted outside St. Mark's, but Bellini, two hundred years earlier, showed us many street vendors. The postcard, newspaper and peanut sellers of today are of ancient lineage but those who demand booths to sell their wares from have been banished to the Molo, a few hundred yards away. As a compensation, they now have electric light and an even greater variety of potential customers.

Would this be a good moment to embark on our study of the History of Venice? It will not be a very profound study: ten minutes should suffice to understand enough of the Venetian character to explain how the marvellous things around us came to be here and nowhere else, and as they are, not otherwise.

VI. A little Venetian history. The founders of Venice took to the islands of the lagoon because they were frightened by events on the mainland. With all the help of all the best historians,

it is hard enough for us to understand what went on in the minds of men who lived a hundred years ago. Of those who lived eighteen hundred years ago, it is impossible and we must content ourselves with the knowledge that fear of something terrible, perhaps a heresy, perhaps the ravages of invading barbarians, drove them to Torcello, to Malamocco and, later, to Rivo Alto, the agglomeration of tiny islands which later became Rialto and, in the thirteenth century, Venice.

The flight started about AD 400 and gradually the refugees began to organise themselves into island communities, each with its representative tribune and all under the authority of the Roman Emperor in Constantinople through his representative in Ravenna. It is generally said that the first Doge was elected in 697 and this fits neatly with the deposing of the last one in 1797, exactly eleven hundred years later: the date was probably some thirty years afterwards but we are not going to split hairs. Thus it can be said that, after some three hundred years of formation, the Republic of Venice was born to endure for eleven hundred years, the first six hundred of which were of almost uninterrupted success. Pepin, the son of Charlemagne, attacked her and was repulsed in 809: the Dalmatians also tried and lived to regret their folly. Until 829, St. Theodore was the patron saint of Venice but he was, still is, too obscure for an up-and-coming state, so the Venetians sent a couple of merchant adventurers to steal the body of St. Mark from Alexandria, deposed St. Theodore and his mysterious crocodile, and built a chapel next to the Doge's Palace to receive their new protector. (According to a German pilgrim writing in 1483, they were duly repaid in their own coin by having St. Mark's body stolen from them and taken to Germany.)

Gradually they learnt how to make a profit out of other people's quarrels and ambitions and, after becoming the ally instead of the vassal of Constantinople, ended by eclipsing her in influence. Their policy was simple: never take sides and always have the best ships in Europe. When the Crusades came, Venice took a little time to realize just how ripe a plum had fallen into her lap, but after the first three, she had gained a great deal of money through ferrying crusaders as well as some valuable Mediterranean ports. Her real coup was yet to come with the Fourth Crusade. Meanwhile, she had built up her prestige sufficiently to receive the Holy Roman Emperor Frederick Barbarossa and Pope Alexander III when, in 1177, they had exhausted each other in their struggles and were ready to make peace. The Pope was so delighted by his reception that he gave the Doge a consecrated ring as a mark of Venice's sovereignty over the sea. The Doge then proceeded in his *Bucintoro*, that magnificent State Barge (named after Alexander the Great's horse, Bucephalus) which we see in so many pictures painted to commemorate great occasions (including Plates 8 and 9), and, having reached the Porto di Lido, he threw the ring into the sea, thus marrying the Adriatic with appropriate phrases. Venice, of course, had never been in any doubt herself as to her sovereignty over the sea and had been performing some such ceremony for many years. Now, though, it had the Pope's blessing and the ceremony was repeated each year until the fall of the Republic. The frugal will be reassured to know that there was great competition to dive in and recover the ring which the finder was allowed to keep.

But it was with the Fourth Crusade in 1202 that Venice showed her now fully developed powers of rapacity, intrigue and hard bargaining. First, she undertook to ship and provision the crusaders for an amount far beyond their capacity to pay and, in addition, half of the booty they might amass from the expedition. Then, when they failed to pay up, she set them to capture some Dalmatian ports for her as a substitute for payment. Finally, she persuaded them to forget the Holy Land altogether and instead capture and sack Constantinople where there were already some 200,000 Venetians making a thorough nuisance of themselves. The sack of Constantinople is unparalleled in history. The city had been the capital of Christian civilization for nine centuries and was filled with works of art of which, perhaps, only the Venetians knew the true value. When the murder, rape and looting were done with, the booty was divided up according to the agreement. A quarter was left for the new Emperor enthroned by the invaders, the rest was divided half and half between the Crusaders and the Venetians whose share included the bronze horses on St. Mark's and much else that we still see in Venice.

There never was a greater crime against humanity than this 'Crusade against Christians' and it had disastrous consequences for the whole western world. Not immediately for Venice, though. She had at last become a great European power and controlled the whole of the Eastern Mediterranean – ' Lords and Masters of a Quarter and a Half Quarter of the Roman Empire', as she described herself. Doge Enrico Dandolo, the almost blind ring-leader of the gangsters, stayed on in Constantinople where he died a year later at the age of ninety-seven, and his successors at home settled down to enjoy the fruits of victory, marred only by the rumblings of Genoa's rivalry which was to prove for so long a thorn in Venetian flesh.

In 1297 an event of great significance occurred

– the six hundred years of government by a democratic monarchy ended and five hundred years of government by the aristocracy began. No longer could an ambitious and commanding Doge become too big for his boots; no longer was there a danger of the masses getting real control of the state. The Grand Council, which had governed completely, was closed down and only members of noble families whose names were inscribed in the Golden Book were eligible for the new Assembly. A complicated system of checks and balances was evolved as a result of which power passed first to a Council of Ten and ultimately to a Council of Three. The Doge was stripped of his powers and the post became one for men of past achievement and future impotence. As time went on his position grew worse. He was forbidden to leave the city for an hour without the consent of the Council. He was not allowed to write a letter, even to his wife, without showing it to one of his six counsellors, or to open one brought to him except in their presence. They had then to read it first and, in the words of a sixteenth-century traveller,

'perhaps deliver it to him, perhaps not'. And the less he had to do, the more he had to show off. He must not speak in the Council or utter anything but platitudes to a visitor, but he must preside over all ceremonies in glorious and extravagant costume, always attended by the nobility.

One Doge, Marin Falier, failed to understand what was expected of him. He tried to exercise some power, was charged with conspiracy against the state and lost his head. The head was shown to the people from the upper arcade of the Doge's Palace and afterwards the two shafts between which the executioner stood to show it were removed and red ones put in their place. They are still there. In place of his portrait in the great Council Chamber, where all the Doges may be seen, there was put a black square. It is still there.

Now began Venice's greatest two centuries. Only Genoa disputed with her for her monopolies and territories, and for fifty years proved troublesome indeed. Genoa almost succeeded in its ambitions against Venice but finally in 1380

The First Doge
Paoluccio Anafesto, 697–717

The Last Doge
Ludovico Manin, 1789–97

the showdown came and Venice fought her last
battle in the lagoon and won it at Chioggia.

With Genoa out of the way, Venice gained
ground on the mainland, up nearly to Trieste
and across to Verona. She had to have free
outlets in the west for the merchandise she had

acquired from the east. Then she went too far
and disputed for Milan. Moreover she abandoned her principle of not taking sides in the
disputes of others and tried siding first with one
contender and then with the other according
to which seemed more advantageous to herself.

The Wickedest Doge
Enrico Dandolo, 1192–1205

The Unluckiest Doge
Marin Falier, 1354–55

By 1500 she was the best hated state in Europe and two terrible things had happened: Constantinople had fallen to the Turks in 1453 and, much worse still, Diaz had rounded the Cape of Good Hope and opened the sea route to the Indies. Venice had a competitor in trade, something she had never known before; it was the acquiring of monopolies which had been her strength, and trading on the follies of others, not competitive trading. She tried meddling in the affairs of Florence and even gave Europe the impression that she was bidding for the domination of Italy when in fact she had enough on her hands with staving off the Turks in the Mediterranean. All Europe united in a 'stop Venice' movement although such unity was too good to last and Venice was left only slightly damaged. But nothing could undo the harm of the new trade routes and the decline had begun.

One source of revenue continued, however, for when profits from the Crusades dried up, Venice found that there was no cause for despair; the Christians' longing to see the holy places and things of the near East could always be turned to good account. Soon the pilgrimages started, and before long Venice's whole fleet was turned over to tourism. She treated her customers well, so long as they paid the price; the richer ones were even granted an audience of the Doge who was concerned that everyone should be satisfied. Guides were provided for the pilgrims to show them where they could buy or hire their necessities for the voyage ahead – changes of clothing, strong perfumes, insecticides, guide books in several languages and manuals of good behaviour, all of which could be bought from the shops round the Piazza, together with rosaries, relics and souvenirs of every description. And the guides were sufficiently well paid by the Senate for tips to be forbidden, particularly commissions from the tradesmen whose shops they visited.

Everything was done to make agreeable the period of waiting in Venice for their ship to be made ready. It is true there was little sightseeing in the form of pictures of saints to be seen in churches – but, better still, there were the saints themselves. Brother Fabri, from Germany, was held up for thirty-one days and occupied his time escorting his fellow pilgrims into at least one church a day, and often several. In the inevitable travel book which followed his return home (they were almost as thick on the ground as they are today) he recounted how they had seen seventeen separate complete bodies, plus many Holy Innocents at Murano, and almost innumerable heads, arms, hands and fingers.

For many centuries, then, the business of Venice had been Business. Now it became Art. Ruskin dates the beginning of the Fall of Venice from the death of Doge Tommaso Mocenigo in

1423 and the succession of Foscari. Maybe, but the following half-century produced Gentile and Giovanni Bellini and Carpaccio, and the half-century after that was still producing men such as Giorgione, Titian, Tintoretto and Veronese. The Foscari and Dario palaces were built after 1423 and the Ca' d'Oro, too. Then came the early Renaissance buildings such as the Miracoli, the inner courtyard of the Doge's Palace, the Clock Tower in the Piazza and the Colleoni statue opposite SS. Giovanni e Paolo – we shall see all these things and may well be able to picture for ourselves something of what Venice looked like during that miraculous fifteenth century.

For two centuries after 1500 the decline of Venice as a power continued and by the time Tiepolo and Canaletto were twenty-one (1718) it had become complete. Nothing remained to her in the Levant but Corfu and a few Dalmatian ports. The great families of merchant adventurers were now mostly living in idleness and poverty on the mainland. Venice had given herself over to pleasure – but she still made it good business. Her pageants and carnivals, her theatres and balls, were as much designed to attract the tourist as to make the Venetians themselves forget past glories. The craving for music, though, was inherent in the Venetian spirit. Almost everyone went to the opera for it was in Venice that the first *public* opera house opened in 1637, at S. Cassiano, dependent not on the favour of princes and noblemen but on audiences who paid for their seats. Monteverdi was brought from Cremona to be Master of the Music of the Republic and remained in charge at St. Mark's for thirty years, living alongside the Basilica in uncomfortable quarters in the *Canonica*. Later, Vivaldi served for forty years at the *Conservatorio* of the Pietà, one of the four schools where orphans and foundlings were raised to careers dedicated wholly to music. Scarlatti and Handel conducted their own operas in Venice, and Tartini, already famous as a violinist, heard Veracini at one of the Mocenigo palaces and decided to start learning his instrument all over again. In the last twenty years of the seventeenth century there were a hundred and fifty operas performed in Venice and ten new ones every year for the next fifty years. 'The chief part they intend to act here is to amuse the rest of Europe and do nothing,' Lord Manchester, the English ambassador, wrote home when he had failed in his mission to persuade the Venetians to enter the war against France in 1708.

The century of play and pleasure ended in 1797 when Napoleon appeared on the scene. At first he was welcomed by some, who saw in him the best hope of achieving their ambition of a united Italy. Soon, though, it was realised that he had sold Venice to the Austrians before he had even conquered it. His price was being left alone for ten years to pursue his other ambitions and as soon as it was promised to him he turned on Venice, for which he had the greatest contempt. She was 'unfit for liberty,' he said, and, later, 'I don't want any more Inquisitors or any more Senate.' The last Doge, Ludovic Manin, abdicated eleven hundred years after the first had been appointed and Napoleon's generals were ordered to hand over the City to the Austrians. But before they left they were,

he directed, to take out everything they did not want the Austrians to have – and to burn the ships they could not remove. Even the Ship of State, the Doge's own *Bucintoro*, was melted down and the French commanding general had a ring made for himself from its treasure. We already know the fate of the four bronze horses.

Except for ten years between 1805 and 1815, when she became part of Napoleon's new kingdom of Italy, Venice had Austrian soldiers in the Piazza until 1866. Then, again, she became a gift, this time by Bismarck to Garibaldi's new Italy as a reward for Italy's support in the Austro-Prussian war.

There was one interval in the seventy years of Austrian domination and it lasted seventeen months. On 22 March 1848 (commemorated by the Calle Lunga 22 Marzo from which the land entrances of the Grand Canal hotels are reached) Daniele Manin, who was no relation to the last Doge, led the Venetians to the capture of the Arsenal, the fleet, and the Piazza and forced the Austrian Governor to abandon the lagoon while he announced the re-establishment of the Republic. A year of disaster and heroism ensued. By April 1849, anyone but Manin and his followers would have realised that they had attempted the impossible, but instead, on 2 April (commemorated by part of the street leading from the Rialto Bridge to the station), the Assembly passed a decree that 'Venice will resist Austria at all costs.' But it was not a matter of cost: the Austrians re-entered the city in August and remained there for another seventeen years, hating and being hated by the Venetians all the time.

Such is the history of Venice in a few words – and, of course, it could be told in very different ones. Seen in the cold light of history it appears as a picture of greed, cruelty and cynicism, but how many nations could look back over eleven hundred years with complacency? The history of Venice has, it must be said, also been written as a record of valour, shrewdness and wise government. Let us content ourselves with studying the city the Venetians built and leave it to the historians to discuss the motives of the builders.

VII. View from the Campanile. It is time we paid our bill and left the Piazza now that we know something of the centre of Venice. Let us, if the atmosphere is clear, see something of the jewel's setting. Let us heed Thomas Coryat who wrote in 1612, 'whatsoever thou art . . . forget not to go to the top of St. Mark's tower before thou comest out of the citie.' We will ascend the Campanile. One advantage the new Campanile has over the old is that it contains a lift. We could perhaps walk up the spiral ramp if we preferred it but we could no longer take a horse up it, as Count Wimpffen, an Austrian friend of Effie Ruskin's during her stay in Venice, is said to have done. The Venetians must have sympathised as they always indulged a perverse love of horsemanship. As long ago as 1292, the Grand Council of the Republic was deciding the precise fine for riding to and fro from Rialto by S. Salvatore to S. Marco, or for horse racing in the Piazza – 25 lire, or 25 lashes in the latter case.

The first thing we notice once we reach the top, is that there are no canals to be seen. We are not the first to make this surprising discovery.

When we first sit in the Piazza after dark, if there is no moon, we will notice that the Procuratie buildings lose a dimension and become like stage scenes painted on canvas. It is mildly irritating to find that this, like the absence of canals from the Campanile, has been noticed by almost every previous visitor to Venice. We must get used to sharing our feelings and discoveries with travellers of the past. Do we feel that so much has been said and written about Venice, not only by learned men, but also by great scholars, that it appears to us there is nothing left to say? If so, we shall be repeating the very words uttered on the subject by Canon Pietro Casola who was in this Piazza on his way to Jerusalem in 1494.

The purpose of making this ascent, which leads to no café, is not to identify as many churches as possible but to see something of the lagoon in which Venice lies. Looking south, first, we see the thin strip of land which cuts it off from the Adriatic. There are, in fact, three strips, called *lidi*, plural of *lido*. The one nearest to us, the middle of the three, was originally called Malamocco but is now called simply The Lido. It was a city when Venice was only a village but all that is left of it is the harbour, still called Malamocco, and not in any case on the site of the old city, and – well, and The Lido. The lagoon is seen to be peppered with islands, most of them with a history of their own. In 1787 Goethe stood on this spot (or, to be accurate, on the equivalent spot of the original Campanile) and saw the sea for the first time in his life. He was already thirty-seven and had for long been the most popular author in Europe. It was high tide in the lagoon and, having seen it in its glory, he later returned to see it 'in its humiliation at low tide'. We may well emulate him and return here when the tide is in the opposite state to its present one.

On the right, although it is probably out of sight, is the mainland and here the waters of the River Brenta emptied themselves into the lagoon at Fusina. They brought so much silt into the lagoon, though, together with that brought by two other rivers on the north side, that the lagoon would have been clogged entirely if nothing had been done. The Venetians therefore built canals to take all the water but a trickle into the Adriatic, south of Chioggia. Thus the lagoon is a salt-water one and the tides, coming in through the gaps between the *lidi* (called *porti*) provide the city's canals with a daily flush – but, from the appearance of many of them, one of decreasing vigour. Many say that this is due to the works of man in the city itself.

Immediately in front of us we see S. Giorgio Maggiore, which by this time we know by sight, and, to the right of it, a long, narrow island called the Giudecca. Behind the Giudecca are three small islands, called La Grazia, S. Clemente and Sacca Sessola. In front of the Giudecca, to the right, we see the entrance to the Grand Canal, dominated by the church of the Salute, and we can, if we wish, retrace our steps from the Molo, through the Piazzetta, to the Piazza. It was from here that, in 1857, James Holland painted the picture reproduced on the cover of this book.

If we now turn to the windows facing, roughly, west, we shall see the Piazza and, in the distance, on the extreme right, the railway and road bridges leading to the mainland, which we can now see clearly, together with the great Breda works to remind us that by no means all Venetians live on the tourists.

We turn, avoiding the postcard counter, and walk round to the east windows. Here we see the Riva degli Schiavoni, with many ships tied up alongside and beyond it the islands of S. Erasmo, La Certosa and Vignole, hard to separate one from the other. Behind them is the main, the only real, entrance to the lagoon, the Porto di Lido, to or from which we shall almost certainly see ships making their way. On the left, if it is clear, we may see the island of Torcello, recognisable from its austere campanile, and of Burano to its right. Far away to the left, if we are lucky, we may even see the snow-capped Alps, and everywhere are channels marked by *pali* for the benefit of shipping. If the tide happens to be out, we are made well aware of their need.

Finally, we turn to the north windows and, looking somewhat to the right, we see, behind the great mass of brick that is the Gothic church of

SS. Giovanni e Paolo, the cemetery island of S. Michele with its cypresses, and, to the left of it, Murano, the island of glass factories. Further to the left is the Dead Lagoon, where the tides never reach.

As for the city, it is, as we see, quite small. The gardens to the east mark its end and we could walk there easily in half an hour. If we knew our way, we could reach the northern boundary as quickly and stand on the frontier to the north lagoon. Below us, to the south, stands the entrance to the Grand Canal and we could see every palace from here to its end in half an hour by the slowest boat. I say we *could* do these things. Come, let's do them.

WALK I

The Accademia,
The Zattere, the Frari, the Rialto Bridge

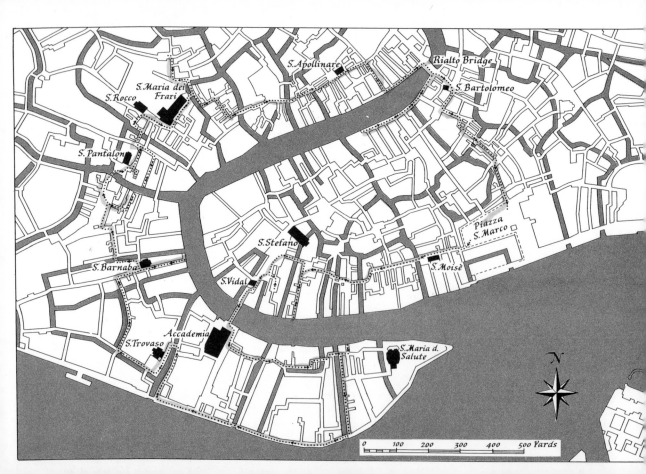

WALK I
The Accademia,
The Zattere, the Frari, the Rialto Bridge

I. Now that we have looked at something of the centre of the city, let us explore the city itself. We shall be surprised to find how quickly we have disengaged ourselves from our fellow tourists. Small though Venice is and inexhaustible as the pleasures it offers are, we shall see few but Venetians once we leave the Piazza, the Mercerie, the Rialto Bridge and the Riva degli Schiavoni.

I will describe but four walks and this will suffice to include almost everything most desirable that the city itself offers – of course, within the limitations already laid down. Three of the walks are long, the remaining one, number 3, quite short. Naturally, it is not intended that the long ones should be completed in a day.

There are several points at which one can break off and return another day. Nevertheless, each can quite easily be done in a day by those who have a limited time in Venice and want to see as much as possible. I may say that I have myself completed each of them in time for a lateish lunch, but this I cannot advise.

Timing is important. Most churches close at midday, the big ones to open again at two-thirty or three, some not until four. Ask the concierge of your hotel who may well have to telephone the church for advice. If you start at nine in the morning, a good time to start, the walks will sort themselves out as far as timing is concerned. Venice in a week? Yes, exactly. One day for the Piazza and surroundings; three for my three long walks; one for walk number 3 with an afternoon to spare; one for a boat trip around the island and to Torcello; one for re-visiting favourites or finding delectabilities I have missed. Venice has always been at her best when taken in fairly small doses – and, of course, you can always come back. And so to walk number 1.

II. Piazza S. Marco to the Accademia.

No traveller will wish to leave Venice without having visited the Accademia. Some will enjoy Venice more after having completed this task than having it ahead of them, so for their benefit we will make it the object of our first expedition beyond the Piazza.

One of the most interesting things about the Accademia is that just outside it lies the only café on the lower reaches of the Grand Canal. A visit would therefore be essential even if the Accademia were not there. And once the contents of the Accademia have been examined, meticulously or perfunctorily according to the visitor's taste, there is an enchanting area of Venice to be seen in its neighbourhood. Let

us therefore resist the temptation to say we did not come to Venice to look at pictures and be off to the Accademia.

We leave the Piazza by the south-west corner. Away on the right of the Calle de l'Ascensione is a bank housed in a thirteenth-century building which was the Hotel Selvadego. On our left was (still is) another hotel called the 'Luna'. Both were for crusaders, some of whom were said to have met no infidels farther south than the Luna, for that, by implication, was as far as they got. Who shall blame them?

If we leave this busy corner and turn left down the Calle Vallaresso we shall reach Harry's Bar and the S. Marco *vaporetto* station; we shall also pass, on the right, a well-known shirt and blouse shop which carries out orders with remarkable speed. If instead of turning left down the Calle Vallaresso we turn right down the Frezzeria we shall be in an old and important shopping street (named after the arrows which were sold there). Byron took lodgings here on his first arrival in Venice in 1816 and promptly cuckolded his host, a draper named Segati; he was still far from the depths of caddishness, though, that he was later to reach in Venice. Off this street, to the left, a small *calle* leads to the Piscina de Frezzaria and the Colomba restaurant, of considerable merit.

We are going to the Accademia, though, not to Harry's Bar or the Colomba restaurant, so we follow the crowd straight along the Calle Seconda de l'Ascensione, which soon becomes the Salizzada S. Moisè, to the Campo S. Moisè. On our left is 'the frightful façade of S. Moisè', as Ruskin described it, 'one of the basest examples of the basest school of the Renaissance', and, while baseness is being considered, the façade of the Bauer Grünwald Hotel across the way may be worth a glance. We may wonder how Moses came to be canonised but my book of saints is silent on the subject. He is by no means the only Jewish saint with a church in Venice, though; he has Jeremiah, Job, Zaccariah and Samuel to keep him company. From now on, we are not in Ruskin's 'paved alley, some seven feet wide where it is widest' but in the Calle Via Larga 22 Marzo, a wide street (for Venice) of modern buildings, built in 1880 and named

in commemoration of the noble and tragic resistance to the Austrian occupiers under Daniele Manin. On 22 March 1848, the Venetian Republic was proclaimed but seventeen months later the Austrians were back in full control and then they remained until 1866. *Calli* to the left off the 22 March lead to the great hotels on the Grand Canal, such as the Europa-Regina and the former Grand (no longer, alas, used as a hotel). At the end, the street swings left, but before following it we glance into the courtyard reached by the *calle* leading off to the right, the Corte de Ca' Michiel. We return to the main street which we follow as it turns right and we reach a bridge across a canal called 'delle Ostreghe' (oysters) with two restaurants and the Bar Ducale, with quite excellent sandwiches. Pauses should always be made on the bridges, particularly those with cafés beside them, for it is from bridges that Venice's true streets, the canals, can be seen. A pause is therefore indicated here although more rewarding views from bridges, and indeed more intriguing canals will be found than this one. It offers one tiny 'sight'

– a view of the window of Ruskin's bedroom at the corner of the building on the other side of the little canal where it joins the Grand Canal. He stayed at what was then the Casa Wetzlar in 1851-52; it is now the Gritti Hotel.

That digression into the Corte de Ca' Michiel was to see where Isabella Teotochi Albrizzi lived and, now that we are comfortably installed, we may consider that remarkable woman for a moment (her own name, Teotochi, betrays her Greek origin). Before Napoleon's arrival in 1797 she conducted one of Venice's two grandest 'salons' at which literary, musical and political lions received the final mark of acceptance. As her 'salon' was her career, she was disinclined to abandon it when her first husband was sent abroad so she arranged for her marriage to be annulled and acquired a new husband, Count Albrizzi. His presence was required only during the marriage ceremony itself, the honeymoon being spent with Isabella's *cicisbeo* or *cavaliere servente*, a peculiarly Italian institution. The cicisbeo was a combination of secretary, footman, lady's-maid, protector and sometimes, though by no means always, lover. He also provided his mistress's husband with freedom to pursue his own inclinations, the husband, as it was said, being the master appointed by the lady's father whereas her *cicisbeo* was the friend of her own choice.

Isabella, like her friendly rival for the leadership of Venetian society, Giustina Michiel, seemed indestructible. We read of her in 1795 taking up a young poet, Ugo Foscolo, who was to become famous. In 1819 she had the privilege of introducing Byron to his last, greatest (and, some think, only) love, Countess Guiccioli. Byron called Isabella the De Staël of Venice ('not at all dissolute as most of the women are') and later in the year reported sadly that she was dying. It was to be another thirteen years, though, before the lights were to be turned out in Venice's two great drawing rooms, both ladies dying in the same year in their late seventies.

Let us finish our coffee and proceed along the short *calle* which leads to the first of three *campi* between the Accademia Bridge and the Piazza, the Campo S. Maria Zobenigo ('o del giglio', of the lily, as it is called). To the left, at the end of the *campo*, are the entrance to the Gritti Palace hotel (Plates 10 and 11) and the *vaporetto* stop. To the right, the church of S. Maria Zobenigo, bracketed with S. Moisè by Ruskin as 'the most remarkable in Venice for their manifestation of insolent atheism'. He must have suffered deeply from its impieties for he saw it every day when staying at the Casa Wetzlar. We may or may not agree about the insolence of the façade but we cannot fail to be fascinated by the relief plans of Zara (which the Venetians had sent the Crusaders to capture for them when they failed to pay up during the Fourth Crusade), Candia (Crete), Padua, Rome (had they hoped to add this to their Empire?), Corfu and Spalato (Split) which are carved on it. A few yards away on the left is a brick building which is all that is left of the campanile; it was pulled down in 1774 just before life became insupportable to it; Barbari (p. 93) shows us that its predecessor had met the same fate by 1500.

We cross the *campo* and, taking the bridge on the right pass into a tiny *campo*, the Campiello della Feltrina, with its celebrated paper shop, the *Legatoria Piazzesi*, then over another bridge and into the Campo S. Maurizio. Before leaving it let us walk down the Calle del Dose (Doge) to the left. At the end is a tiny *fondamenta* (a walk beside the banks of a canal, so called because it serves as a foundation to the houses). This (the Fondamenta S. Maurizio) is the only one of its kind on the Grand Canal and offers us a convenient vantage point from which we can contemplate the life of the Canal in solitude. It will always be our object to contemplate the palaces of the Grand Canal from dry land where possible rather than from the water. It is easier to read our guide book under such conditions, if that is what we want to do; it is easier to take our photographs. Above all, we can keep our heads in one position and not have to turn from side to side as do our fellow tourists on their *vaporetto*, for all the world as if they were at Wimbledon.

We can see nothing of our own side of the Canal from our little *fondamenta* but opposite us we can see the whole range from the Salute to the Accademia Bridge which we shall soon be crossing. Opposite us is the ground floor of what was to have been the huge house of the Veniers, but this was as high as they got and the unfinished palace was abandoned for two hundred years. Mrs Peggy Guggenheim then bought it and since her death it has become a museum for her collection of modern pictures. Next to it (towards the Salute) was another Venier palace, replaced by a modern house, and next to that the Palazzo Dario which seems about to disintegrate and fall into the canal. It was built about 1450 and is a typical example of the Venetians' love of bright coloured marble. The Dario is one of the best beloved of all the Grand Canal palaces.

Looking towards the right, we see the little Campo S. Vio on the corner of which is the Palazzo Barbarigo, once (and perhaps still?) occupied by the Venezia Murano Glass Company. They had those mosaics put there in 1883, not, as one might have thought, as a warning but as an advertisement of their wares. It had been an ancient palace and Canaletto's picture opposite shows its side façade. He painted it often: Plate 13 is another version, without the man on the roof cleaning the chimney – an excessively difficult operation with Venetian chimneys. The tiny chapel was built in 1864 and replaced a fourteenth-century church which achieved importance because a rebellion happened to be put down on the name day of its saint. Consequently, the Doge visited it annually in state to give thanks – and went on doing so until the fall of the Republic four hundred years later. On the far side of the canal (the Rio S. Vio) are two seventeenth-century palaces, the Loredan and the Balbi-Valier, then a garden and then the Palazzo Contarini dal Zaffo (one of twenty-two palaces called 'Contarini' but the Contarinis were quite a family. One of them was there when the first Doge was elected in 697 and the family provided eight Doges themselves.) Restored though it be, this is a palace worth looking at and, perhaps, it is worth comparing its façade with that of the Dario palace lower down the Grand Canal.

We now leave our private little *fondamenta* and return to the top of the Campo S. Maurizio. The

leaning campanile we see ahead is that of S. Stefano, although it is much nearer the church of S. Maurizio. We shall see a lot of this landmark. We follow the *calle* to the left, over a bridge to the right of which we can see how the canal goes under the church of S. Stefano, and so reach the Campo S. Stefano.

This huge *campo* was a great place for bullfights and carnivals and we may well take coffee at the café at its entrance and contemplate the palaces which surround it. Three of them are called, respectively, Palazzo Barbaro, Loredan and Morosini but here one is confronted with a recurring difficulty in following the names of Venetian palaces for there are three other Barbaros, eight other Loredans and twelve other Morosinis among the palaces. The pure pleasure lover in Venice, therefore, may well ignore the names of all but the best-known palaces and, of course, those which particularly take his fancy. The Pisani Palace, though, off a little *campo* named after it on the left, at the canal end of the Campo S. Stefano, is worth walking to. It is the Conservatory of Music (not one of the original

four) and hideous sounds emanate from it, but its inner courtyards with their pillars of Istrian stone which were the status symbol of its ancient owner are strangely impressive – if you can get inside to see them.

Returning to the Campo S. Stefano we turn left and go round the church of S. Vidal to the Campo S. Vidal. On our left, then, are the gardens of the Cavalli or Franchetti Palace, a monster of unsympathetic restoration, named after its perpetrator, Baron Franchetti. In front of us is the Accademia Bridge and, before we examine it, we may care to pop into the Art Gallery which the church has become, where we might if we are very deserving, be allowed to see the Carpaccio of S. Vitale (the same saint, of course) on horseback. This diversion, though, is strictly for Carpaccio lovers.

Let us now turn our eyes to the Grand Canal and manoeuvre ourselves into the position from which Canaletto's *Stonemason's Yard* (opposite) was painted – we do so by studying the angle of the church of the Carità, now the Accademia, on the far side of the Grand Canal and getting

as far away from it as possible against the wall of the church of S. Vidal.

The first thing we notice is that there is no longer a campanile to the Carità. It fell down in 1744 destroying the houses in front of it and, unlike a number of fallen Venetian campanili, it has never been replaced. Next we notice that the house on the right of the picture is still there. We are, indeed, standing beside it. Looking across the Grand Canal, again, we see that the campanile of S. Trovaso (for that is the name of the church) has lost its dome but is otherwise unaltered. The house immediately to the right of the campanile is also unchanged; it is now the British Consulate and the Queen looked out of that window when she visited Venice in 1962. This great picture shows Canaletto at the top of his form and painting as if every shaft of light on each brick was a new discovery. He painted many fine pictures but few undoubted masterpieces and those of us who live in London are fortunate indeed that our National Gallery owns three of these (see p. 98 for another). Until a few years ago there was,

amazingly, no Canaletto view on exhibition in all Venice, only the capriccio he gave the Accademia when ultimately elected. This has now been rectified by the city having acquired two of his finest and earliest paintings which are on exhibition at the Ca' Rezzonico (see p. 95).

We may now turn our attention to the great wooden structure of the Accademia Bridge, unknown to both Canaletto and Ruskin. It is a temporary one only. It will be replaced by a stone bridge as soon as the Municipality can afford it, so they say. It has been there for over seventy years, though, and itself replaced an extremely ugly iron bridge which was built in 1854. That in turn was the result of good intentions coming to nothing. A single-arch stone bridge had been contemplated in 1838 to commemorate the accession of Ferdinand I of Austria, and a writer of the day wrote that it was doubtful whether the loss in point of scenic effect or the gain to the city would preponderate. In any case nothing happened until 1854 and then it was that truly dreadful iron affair. Ruskin found it there when he returned in 1876 and thought it 'ghastly'. He particularly resented the toll which was used to pay the English builders of the bridge and thought the money would have been better spent, as in his day, on the gondoliers operating the ferry service. They, as a result of the bridge, had had to take to begging, drinking and bellowing – but everything was going to pieces since the introduction of steam.

If the iron bridge had not been too low for the new type of *vaporetto* to sail under, it would no doubt still be there, but by 1933 a new bridge was essential, both here and at the station, where a similar iron bridge had been built at the same time. Both the new bridges were designed by the same architect and both, indeed, follow the same design. The station bridge, however, was built in stone since the Canal is far narrower there and stone could be afforded, whereas here the builders had to make do with wood. It is surprising what a difference the two materials make to the appearance.

As for the displaced gondoliers, they still have a hard time. Gondolas are expensive to maintain and few tourists can afford to hire them for their sightseeing. There are only seven *traghetti* (gondola ferries) left so the gondoliers have to rely largely on the nightly serenade.

Let us ascend the bridge and stop soon after its highest point. It is a commanding scene, indeed. Looking down the Grand Canal, towards the Salute but on the left, next to the Palazzo Cavalli, we see a pair of palaces built by the Barbaro family – the family who paid for the façade of S. Maria Zobenigo which so disgusted Ruskin and who had it devoted entirely to the glorification of their somewhat bloodthirsty exploits. 'So they have been brought to their garrets justly,' commented Ruskin to his father after he and Effie had dined with tenants in the palace's state rooms while two old brothers, the last of the Barbaros, were living in one of the garrets on the fourth floor. In the last century it was bought by a family named Curtis who used to place its 'large, cool upper floor' at the disposal of Henry James ('£40 a year to anyone but me,' he wrote to a friend). He loved Venice ('I don't care if I never see Rome or Florence again,' he added) and he loved the Barbaro so much that he resisted the temptation of buying a little house of his own, complete with garden, higher up the Grand Canal, which was offered at an absurdly cheap price. He repaid the Curtises' hospitality by placing the climax of *The Wings of the Dove* in the Palazzo Barbaro and perhaps exorcising the memories of the Barbaro family.

At the end we see the side of the huge stone Palazzo Corner della Ca' Grande ('one of the worst and coldest buildings of the Central Renaissance' was, of course, Ruskin's comment); it is a landmark which can be seen from the extreme east of the city. Then the grand hotels begin just as the Canal bends round. On the right, we see the Venier and Dario palaces which we saw from the Fondamenta S. Maurizio.

Looking up the canal, we can see only as far as the Palazzo Rezzonico on the left. A tablet records that Robert Browning died there, which is true, and every gondolier and most guide books will tell you that he owned it, which is not. In fact, it had been bought in 1887 by his unpromising son, Pen, who had just married an American heiress, to Browning's delight. Pen immediately set about restoring and redecorating the gigantic building with such success that Henry James wrote home 'what he has done here with the splendid Palazzo Rezzonico transcends description for beauty'. Two years later, Browning caught cold on a visit to Pen and died; soon afterwards the American heiress could bear neither the 'stately temple of the rococo' nor Pen any longer and left, determined to become an Anglican nun. The palace had one more private owner and then, in 1935, it was sold to the Municipality who furnished it from the many eighteenth-century possessions of the Correr Museum (see p. 95). Fortunately for us, the amateurs' cameras were already clicking in Venice and the Brownings posed for their friend Miss Barclay outside the palace with the result shown opposite.

There are two Gothic palaces between the Rezzonico and the Accademia, the Loredan and the Contarini dagli Scrigni, and then comes the British Consul's house. On the right there are no

palaces of particular note. (I should mention here that Ca' is short for Casa, or house, and that there is no significance between its use and that of the grander Palazzo as a prefix. Some very grand palaces, such as the Ca' d'Oro, are never called Palazzo; some very modest houses seem always to enjoy the name. Most of them are called by either name, just as the speaker chooses.)

It is time to descend the bridge. On our right stands the Accademia. On our left the café. We resolutely turn right.

III. The Accademia. The first nineteen rooms of the Accademia can be done in half an hour by any traveller with sound limbs and a willingness to postpone the delights of such heavyweights as Titian, Tintoretto and Veronese (those who came to Venice expressly to see the work of these masters will need several visits to the Accademia; they will also need to enter many dark churches in pursuit of their goal).

Room I can be walked through quickly with an admiring glance at the floor and ceiling. Room II has two Giovanni Bellinis, one painful and one with a lovely background, two Carpaccios, including a famous *Presentation*, and three Cimas: *Doubting Thomas*, a familiar-looking *Madonna of the Oranges* and a third to be avoided at all costs. Room III need not detain us but in Rooms IV and V (really one room) we are held up badly, first by a stunning *St. George* by Mantegna, then by some glorious small Giovanni Bellinis and a Piero della Francesca *St. Jerome* (all St. Jeromes seem to be enchanting but wait till you see Carpaccio's another day). It also contains that mysterious and irresistible *Tempest* by Giorgione, one of the few Giorgiones never to have had its attribution assailed. Room VI leads straight to Room X without having to pass through Rooms VII, VIII and IX, and advantage should be taken of this fact except for a peep into Room VIII for Bonifacio de' Pitati's *Eternity* (number 917) which gives us a little view of the Piazza as it was in 1533.

On arriving at Room X we find ourselves before Veronese's *Feast at the House of Levi*, about which a book could be written. Ruskin said you must not stop at it for you can see the like of it,

and better, at the Louvre in his *Marriage at Cana*, but we are in Venice, not Paris, and must stop at it. It was painted as a *Last Supper* and Veronese was hauled before the Inquisition, which was sitting for the purpose in a chapel in St. Mark's. The buffoons, dogs, drunkards and dwarfs in the picture had affronted them but above all it was the Germans they could not stomach. 'Were you commissioned to paint Germans in this picture?' they asked. No, answered Veronese, but the picture was very large and there had to be a lot of figures in it. 'Was it fitting that he should paint Germans at our Lord's last supper?' they pressed, and the artist could but answer, 'No, my lord.' Veronese sounded very penitent and ended by saying he did not defend his action. He was given three months in which to correct the picture but he found a less arduous way of satisfying honour all round. He just retitled it *Feast at the House of Levi* instead of *The Last Supper* and left in the dogs, drunkards, dwarfs – yes, and even the Germans. Veronese himself is leaning against a pillar on the left in the foreground.

Room XI has another Veronese and Tiepolo's

Plates 1 & 2: The greatest constellation of beauty in all Europe (p. 17): the Doge's Palace and the Molo looking towards the Salute

Plates 3 & 4: We are on Venice's threshold . . . We are in the Piazzetta (p. 30)

Plates 5 & 6:
Mr. Clark could even see through
it to the Giants' Staircase in the
Courtyard. It was at the head of
these stairs that the Doge stood
to be crowned. . . (p. 47)

Plate 7 (overleaf): There opens a
great light, and in the midst of it
the vast tower of St. Mark seems
to lift itself visibly forth from the
level field of chequered stones. . .
(p. 47)

Plates 8 & 9: The Doge then proceeded in his Bucintoro, *that magnificent State Barge. . .(p. 53): the Molo on Ascension Day*

Plates 10 & 11: From the Campo S. Maria Zobenigo: left, the land entrance to the Gritti Palace; right, the Salute; in the distance, the Riva degli Schiavoni (p. 71)

Plates 12 & 13: The little Campo S. Vio on the corner of which is the Palazzo Barbarigo. Canaletto's picture shows the side façade. He painted it many times. Left, the Palazzo Corner della Cà Grande. Right, the Salute. In the distance, the Riva degli Schiavoni (p. 72)

Plates 14 & 15: The Fondamenta della Zattere, Venice's sunny, sheltered southern promenade (p. 92). Right, the Salute; centre, the Dogana

last fresco cycle. The three rooms leading off the first corridor include a w.c. and smoking area, and the corridor itself has some charming pictures by Marco Ricci, Giuseppe Zais and Zuccarelli as well as three doors which deserve more than a glance. From here we make for the next room which contains examples of a pair of capriccios of which more than fifty versions exist. Which, if any, is by Canaletto himself is almost anyone's guess – certainly not this pair. There are works by the *vedutisti* (eighteenth-century view painters) and by Pietro Longhi which tell us something of what social life was like at the time.

In the same room is Canaletto's *Capriccio of a Colonnade opening on to a Courtyard* which he presented to the Accademia after his long-delayed election in 1763. It is in fact dated 1765, two years after his election, and there is good reason to believe that he first intended the Accademia to have a view (now in Los Angeles) but that view painting was regarded as an inferior form of art, inappropriate to an Academician.

There is also a painting of *The Rio dei Mendicanti and the Scuola di S. Marco* which, the information sheet says, 'most critics now attribute to Bellotto'. Not this one. Belotto was Canaletto's nephew and worked in his uncle's studio from the age of fifteen until his early twenties. He then became an artist of great distinction, working in northern Italy, Dresden and Warsaw – but while in Venice he painted, or assisted in painting, only versions of Canaletto's subjects and it has not been suggested that he composed any pictures but this one, although he may well have painted much, perhaps all, of it. There are several viewpoints in the picture which is full of subtleties I cannot believe Bellotto was capable of at that time (*c.* 1740). Ruskin knew the painting when it was in a private Venetian collection and later wrote to a friend 'It's a great Canaletto view and I'm painting it against him'. His drawing, not painting, of the scene exists and is a competent, if pedestrian, picture of the scene from a single viewpoint, lacking all Canaletto's finesse.

We now make for Room XX which has a series

Plate 16: The church opposite is Palladio's Redentore. Every July they build a bridge of boats across the Giudecca canal to commemorate deliverance from a plague.(p. 92)

of paintings by various artists which were commissioned by the Scuola di S. Giovanni Evangelista. This *Scuola*, or Guild, was well endowed. They owned, and still own, the most beautiful little courtyard in Venice, near the Frari (see p. 103) and a Holy Cross which was carried round Venice every year and put through its paces, so to speak: it was made to demonstrate its power to perform miracles. These pictures show some of the miracles it performed. Glancing round at them, to use Ruskin's own words, you see a series of pictures of street architecture with various more or less interesting transactions going on in the streets. Large Canalettos, in fact; only with the figures a little more interesting than Canaletto's figures. And of Gentile Bellini's contribution, the *Procession Round the Piazza Bearing the Cross*, you can only know the value after good study of St. Mark's itself (I have been quoting Ruskin again).

But we who have sat in the Piazza with its pale reproduction, and examined its true viewpoint (p. 44), will recognize the value of this marvellous picture instantly and probably be bowled over by it. We are *in* the Piazza and it is 1498, when Venice was still almost at the height of her power and fortunes. There is that mosaic over the left door of St. Mark's, exactly as it is now and the others as they were, so that we know what we have lost. The Clock Tower is not yet built and the crockets, canopies and pinnacles of St. Mark's are gleaming with gold. So, from the glimpse we get of it, is the Porta della Carta – it is too much to hope that we shall ever see this again, however complete the restorations. The gold on the Porta della Carta is still fresh, for barely sixty years have passed since it had been built. The corner we can see of the Doge's Palace (the columns without bases) is only a few years older. The Acre pillars are there, so is the Pietra del Bando, so are the bronze horses. The Procuratie Nuove have not yet been built so that the right side of the Piazza closes in the Campanile. Someone seems to be roasting a lamb in the Piazzetta dei Leoncini, and isn't that man just outside St. Mark's selling postcards?

Gentile Bellini never attained the stature of his

younger brother, Giovanni, although it was he who had been sent to Constantinople when Mehmet II had asked for the best portrait painter in Venice in 1479. He made another contribution to the S. Giovanni Evangelista cycle, showing a miracle taking place after the cross had fallen into the water of the Rio S. Lorenzo. The canal leads off the Riva degli Schiavoni and we shall see the spot where Gentile Bellini stood for his picture. And so to Carpaccio's miracle which is taking place at the Rialto Bridge.

Carpaccio was a very different painter from either of the Bellini brothers, although some say he learnt the science of perspective from one of them. Others believe he never did learn perspective as a science but merely painted what he saw. It is Carpaccio's incidental figures and episodes that are so endearing; there is always a dog, or a nurse or someone writing or arguing in some corner of the picture, to remind us that Carpaccio was first a reporter and that he would have been just as happy painting scenes like Canaletto's instead of saints and legends if he had lived in a day when it was fashionable to paint such things. He had the misfortune to live at the end of an era rather than the beginning of one. The New Art of Titian, Tintoretto and Veronese burst on Venice towards the end of his life with the explosiveness of the Impressionists four hundred years later, but to many of us those painters are men we respect whereas Carpaccio is the one we love.

The Miracle of the Holy Cross at the Rialto Bridge is a prelude to what awaits us in the next room. It was probably painted in 1494, just before the present bridge was built, and already the timbers are rotting. The Patriarch of Grado had just come out on to the balcony of his palace below the Bridge to drive the demon out of an unfortunate supplicant – and has succeeded. We are looking up the Grand Canal, where we shall be this very day, and some of the buildings on the right, such as the Ca' da Mosto and the campanile of S. Giovanni Crisostomo are still there. All were there in Carpaccio's time, except the Patriarch's balcony, which is imaginary. In case we refer to this picture later when we know the scene better and seek the Fondaco dei

Tedeschi (the present Post Office) we should note that that building was not begun until 1507 and, even if 1494 is a premature date for the picture, it was certainly painted before 1505. However tempting it is, therefore, to call the building on the extreme right the Fondaco dei Tedeschi, we have to admit that it is not in the picture. What is in, though, is the sign of the Sturgeon Hotel, a popular hostel for both crusaders and pilgrims and well spoken of in guide books of the fifteenth century, of which there were quite a number. You can see the sign on this side of the bridge, just past the Patriarch's Palace. If you look closely you can see someone by the Grand Canal, below the balcony on which the miracle is being wrought, standing with a little bag round his neck and the arms of his *Scuola* on it. It was his job to collect the guttering wax from any candles that might have been used and to put it in his little bag.

The other miracles do not keep up the standard set by Gentile Bellini and Carpaccio, and Room XXI awaits us. The Accademia has provided us with a crescendo of beauty. The burst into fortissimo is about to take place. We must peep in, although whether to stay and look or to put the whole thing aside for a morning or afternoon's wallowing is for each of us to decide according to his taste.

The St. Ursula series, for that is what Room XXI contains, was painted by Carpaccio for another *Scuola*, this time the Scuola di S. Orsola (St. Ursula) itself. It no longer exists, which perhaps is fortunate, for we can enjoy the pictures here with the benefit of overhead lighting and ease of examination. Another day, we shall be able to see another series of *Scuola* paintings by Carpaccio in the building for which they were painted, the Scuola S. Giorgio degli Schiavoni (very near the S. Lorenzo canal in Gentile Bellini's picture in Room XX). They are not in the very *room* for which they were originally intended. It is, however, near enough for us to be able to decide for ourselves whether we prefer to sacrifice comfort for the original atmosphere. This is the sort of thing art scholars were able to argue for hours when nearly all Carpaccio's pictures were gathered together for an exhibition in the Doge's Palace in 1963. Art Gallery or Church (or *Scuola*)? A pretty point. But let's look at the pictures.

For once, and once only, I propose to tell the story of the pictures. As works of art, they speak for themselves but they *were* painted to tell a story and, as comparatively few of those who look at them know what the story is, it would be useful to have it on hand, for use now or later.

Ursula was the daughter of the Christian King of – and already we are in trouble. She had been born wrapped in a hairy mantle, hence her name Ursula, little bear. By the time she was fifteen her beauty and wisdom had become known abroad and a heathen king wanted her as wife to his son. Whose daughter? Which heathen king? Nearly all the books agree that she was the King of Britain's daughter and that the heathen king was of England. This makes no sense and some make the foreigner a pagan king 'from abroad', some from Ireland. The easiest course for us to follow is to treat Ursula as a Princess of Brittany rather than Britain and allow that England was the heathen country (after all,

England was not converted by St. Augustine until 600 and the Huns' invasion, which we are to see depicted in the legend, was complete by 453).

And so it was, for us, the King of England who sent an embassy of noblemen to Brittany to make his proposal and also to make it clear that, if it were not accepted, he intended to follow and take Ursula away himself. This is the subject of the first picture which is divided into three parts. The first part, on the left, shows Venice and is there as a compliment to the benefactors of the Scuola of St. Ursula who had commissioned the series from Carpaccio. In the middle part the Ambassadors are being given audience, and here is an interesting thing. There is a blank rectangle at the bottom of the picture, obviously to allow for the top of a door over which it was to be hung. The pictures were hung in the Oratory of the *Scuola* but, until recently, no one knew quite how they had been hung. Someone then thought of studying the Barbari view (page 148) carefully and not only found the Oratory but worked out the position each picture occupied.

Research can still be carried on, in Venice at any rate, without the use of computers and X-rays. To return to the first picture, though: at the right, the King is showing his anxiety at the idea of his daughter marrying a heathen prince, but Ursula sees it as a chance to do missionary work and persuades him to agree on condition the young prince becomes a Christian and that there should be an engagement of three years spent on a pilgrimage accompanied by eleven maidens as her companions (legend has turned the eleven into eleven thousand, but this is generally thought to be due to misreading 'Ursula et XI.M.V', which means Ursula and eleven virgin martyrs, as Ursula and 11,000 virgins).

In the second picture the Ambassadors are receiving the King's answer, a scribe being employed to put everything in writing to avoid misunderstanding.

In the third, the Ambassadors have returned to England (it seems remarkably like Venice and, indeed, parts of it are recognisably Venice, but no matter). The heathen King is dealing with some other matter than his son's future and the Prince is asking the arriving Ambassador the result of his mission without waiting for him to be called to the King's presence. According to Ruskin, the Ambassador is telling the Prince to be patient until the King is ready, but I do not know his authority for this.

The next picture is also in three parts. On the left the Prince is taking leave of his father and, on the right of the flagpole, he is being greeted by Ursula. On the extreme right, the young couple are bidding farewell to Ursula's father before embarking.

In the fifth picture, Ursula is asleep and an Angel appears to her in her dream. He may be preparing her for the approaching disaster, but it could also be that this picture should really come second in the series and that it depicts Ursula being told to accept the proposal of marriage and convert the heathens of England. The latter was Ruskin's view but he was mad on this picture – for twenty-five years metaphorically, studying it, writing about it and copying it, then literally. The doctors said his mental breakdown had been due to overwork, he wrote to a friend after recovering. But the doctors knew nothing, he added: 'I went crazy about St. Ursula.' Oddly enough, Ruskin had scarcely heard of Carpaccio when he wrote *The Stones of Venice* and did not 'discover' him until twenty years later.

Next we are in Rome, and Ursula, her Prince and her maidens (more than eleven, but fewer than eleven thousand), are being received by the Pope.

The Pope himself now decided to join the pilgrimage, taking bishops, priests and even some cardinals with him. The seventh picture shows us the whole party arriving at Cologne, the land of the Huns, but this was the first picture in the series which Carpaccio painted and he had not yet quite got into his stride.

And now the tragedy. Under the walls of Cologne, the party is set upon by the Huns. They could have saved themselves, but only by denying their God, and Ursula preferred death for them all. A pity, thought the son of the King of the Huns, as he stood by watching the archer about to plunge the arrow into the beautiful young saint. He had fallen in love, as everyone did, with Ursula, but she was destined for Paradise and, on the right of the picture, her bier is being carried by the bishops.

The last picture shows her having reached her final destination, but Paradise looks a dull place compared with what we have seen of England and Brittany – and there is no sign of the bridegroom.

We can take no more beauty and fortunately there is little left to take. Room XXIII is generally closed unless there is an exhibition but it used to contain one curiosity, all that remains of Giorgione's long-perished frescos from the Fondaco dei Tedeschi. Now this wraith has been removed to the Ca' d'Oro where it may be wondered at in Venice's newest museum by those with the eye of faith (p. 173). Room XXIV has a glorious ceiling and Titian's *Presentation of the Virgin*, 'stupid and uninteresting', wrote Ruskin.

There is now nothing between us and that café on the Grand Canal. We get back to Room I and so out to buy our postcards, and into the sunshine. We have done the Accademia.

IV. The Grand Canal seen from the Accademia. With the Accademia behind us we shall be able to enjoy the spectacle of the Grand Canal from the café far more than if we had turned left immediately when descending the Accademia Bridge. We shall also be able to look at the inevitable postcards we have bought and may even find time to put in some study of the ACTV services. Before doing so, we glance up the Grand Canal. From the bridge, we could see no further than the Ca' Rezzonico, but now a few more palaces have appeared beyond it. The first is the Palazzo Bernardo, but there are two finer palaces of this name, one of them further up the Grand Canal. Then come a group of three palaces called Giustinian of which the further two are Gothic. In 1858, Wagner, after a night in 'a gloomy lodging' in the Danieli Hotel, found the middle one to let. He had his luggage quickly transferred there, sent for his Erard Grand, said to himself, 'At last I am living in Venice,' and settled down to complete *Tristan*. The Giustiniani were great swells, even in Venice where swells abounded. There were certainly Giustiniani around in the eighth century, although perhaps not, as the family claim, at the foundation of Athens. In the twelfth century there was a momentary danger that Venice would have to continue without Giustiniani, the only one left being a monk in a monastery on the Lido; all the rest had been killed either by plague or battle while the Venetians were wintering on the island of Chios during one of their wars against the infidels. The situation was untenable and the Pope was beseeched by the people of Venice to release young Nicolo Giustiniani from his vows. Permission granted, the young man was married to the Doge's daughter who produced nine sons and three daughters for him. He then returned to his cloister and his wife founded a nunnery, leaving the children to propagate – which they did effectively, for by the sixteenth century there were fifty different branches of the family and there are today twelve Giustinian palaces in Venice, one of them being the Europa Hotel.

The next palace is also really a Giustinian; at any rate they built it, but it was bought by the

Foscaris whose name it has borne ever since the fifteenth century. It has been mightily restored but is nevertheless the most important Gothic palace on this reach of the Grand Canal. When Ruskin first went to Venice it was a foul ruin, its hall a sea of mud (but the 'noblest example of the Gothic' all the same). On his last visit, it had been restored by the Venetians and given to the Austrians for use as a barracks (at least, Ruskin said it was 'given'; one wonders). Now it is part of the University.

Between the Ca' Foscari and the Renaissance Palazzo Balbi (the one with obelisks) farther up the Canal runs the Rio Nuovo, the 'new' canal leading to the station. The Palazzo Balbi's claim to distinction, apart from its unique position *in volta del canal* (at the canal's turn), is that the Balbi who built it adopted an unusual method of making the builders hurry: he swore that he would sleep under no roof until it was finished and moored a boat outside. He kept his word but caught cold and died before the work was done. Napoleon saw the regatta from this palace and the judges' stand has always been erected outside

it. Its obelisks make it easily recognisable in pictures, such as the one overleaf. Next door to it in the Rio Nuovo is an undistinguished house with probably the best view in all Venice, a site ripe for development indeed. Already sixty years ago, E. V. Lucas was remarking that 'it might be made so desirable'. The problem is, what can one build on it? Frank Lloyd Wright was quite uninhibited by the neighbourhood and produced what some thought an admirable solution in the fifties. It caused such a sense of shock, however, among the Venetian traditionalists that permission to rebuild was refused and the site remains as it was.

V. Between the Accademia and the Zattere. Now we really can take our coffee, and after it we can start our walk. I promise to write as little as possible while we are walking; nothing is worse than having to read a guide book while walking and looking round, all at the same time. Comments will therefore be reserved for when we are sitting down and, so far as possible, only the minimum of directions for

when we need to get from one place to another. They may even be too minimal and we may get lost. No matter. Accost the first passer-by without a camera, smile and say, for example, 'Zattere?' His answer will be '*sempre dritto*' (straight on), which will not help much as nothing is straight on in Venice. He will, however, add gestures to his answer which will, at any rate, set us off in the right direction. In all probability, he will insist on personally escorting us, whether he happened to be going in our direction or not. If he does not answer '*sempre dritto*', he is not a Venetian and his directions must be treated with caution; he may be just another Englishman showing off by walking about Venice without a camera. Venetians *always* answer '*sempre dritto*'. James Morris, by far the city's best twentieth-century chronicler, tells us (in *Venice* [Faber 1983]) how Pepin attempted to take Venice in 809 and reached Malamocco, which the Venetians had abandoned in favour of the group of islands called Rivo Alto – Rialto. 'Only one old woman had stayed behind in Malamocco, determined to do or die, and this patriotic crone was summoned to the royal presence. "Which is the way to Rivo Alto?" demanded Pepin, and the old woman knew her moment had come. Quavering was her finger as she pointed across the treacherous flats . . . tremulous was her voice as she answered the prince. "*Sempre dritto*," she said: and Pepin's fleet, instantly running aground, was ambushed by the Venetians and utterly humiliated.' So it has been ever since.

Now that we have confidence, we can finish our coffee and then we turn our backs on the Grand Canal and walk a few yards down the *calle* in which the café stands, the Rio Terrà Foscarini, and immediately turn left along the Calle Nova S. Agnese (signpost: English Church). We cross a canal and are in the Campo S. Vio. Where the man in that smart hat is standing in Plate 12 there was for many years a petrol pump. The man having his siesta on the ground may well still be there, though, or at any rate his descendant. We promise ourselves to return to the little Protestant church next Sunday and proceed along the Calle de la Chiesa to the Fondamenta Venier dai Leoni. We pass the back door of Mrs

Guggenheim's palace and reach the Campiello Barbaro with its three acacia trees and its invitation to artists to reach for the drawing board. The palace whose back stands on the north side of the *campiello* is the Palazzo Dario, surprisingly different in period and type from the Grand Canal façade.

We continue in the direction we were following turning left, then right down Ramo Barbaro, across a canal with two *fondamente*, and after a few yards we can turn left (towards the *traghetto*) for another view of the Grand Canal. We can now see all the great hotels proclaiming their names, with the Gritti Palace immediately opposite and the well-kept *traghetto* station of S. Maria Zobenigo o del Giglio alongside. The vast stone palace to their left is the Palazzo Corner della Ca' Grande, now the Prefecture. Its owner was so intent that it should remain the biggest on the Grand Canal that it was he who stopped Mrs Guggenheim's predecessors from completing the Palazzo Venier dai Leoni in the eighteenth century. The palace with the exquisite balconies, three palaces to the right of the Gritti Hotel, is

called the Contarini-Fasan (Fasan = pheasant: the owner liked shooting them. A more far-fetched legend calls it Desdemona's house, no one knows why.) Ruskin called it 'one of the principal ornaments of the very noblest reach of the Grand Canal' and drew it lovingly. It is worth comparing this section of the Grand Canal with the detail from the Barbari view opposite.

Now we go back to the calle with two *fondamente* and turn left down one of them, the Ca' Bala. This brings us out on the Fondamenta delle Zattere, Venice's sunny, sheltered southern promenade (*zattere* are rafts: timber rafts used to be floated over here from the mainland and moored here). We are on the Giudecca Canal and across the water is the Giudecca Island: the church opposite is Palladio's Redentore (Plate 16). Every July they build a bridge of boats across the Giudecca Canal to the Redentore to commemorate deliverance from a plague.

If we are exhausted we can now turn left and follow the *fondamenta* to the Punta della Dogana (the Custom House Point; Plates 14 and 15),

with probably the most spectacular view in Venice, and from there to the *vaporetto* or *traghetto* stop from the Salute to S. Marco. Better perhaps, though, to reserve this for an evening excursion and, if we are feeling strong, turn right.

The first church we pass is Spirito Santo with its *Scuola* next to it (this is where the bridge of boats starts) and next to that is a new block of flats of interest to those who wonder whether it really is possible to build well in Venice in the language of today; many will feel this is successful. Soon comes the Pensione Calcina, the only spot in Venice with a memorial to Ruskin, although by the time he stayed there he was already suffering from intermittent madness and did no work worth while. Neither the Danieli nor the Gritti Hotels, in which he wrote respectively the first and second volumes of *The Stones of Venice*, pay him any acknowledgment.

If it is nearly lunch-time do not pause at any of the inviting cafés on the Zattere: there will be a good place to lunch in about ten minutes. Otherwise, the cafés may well be patronized. There are few in Venice better sited climatically

and I have drunk Campari outside one of them on Christmas morning.

We next pass the church of the Gesuati, not to be confused with the Gesuiti (Jesuits) in the north of the city, and at the next bridge, the Ponte Longo, we turn right along the Fondamenta Nani by the side of the Rio di S. Trovaso with its much painted and photographed *squero* (boat-building yard). We turn left over the first bridge and then left again and so back along the other side of the Rio to the Campo S. Trovaso (shortened, inexplicably, from SS. Gervasio e Protasio) with its fine old wellhead. After crossing the campo, we turn right along the Fondamenta Bonlini and right again along the Fondamenta di Borgo by the side of the Rio de le Romite. The promised luncheon place appears at last; it is the Locanda Montin on the right and I can only hope it is fine enough to lunch in the garden.

After lunch, we emerge and turn right, continuing along the Fondamenta del Borgo, over a bridge and so to the Calle Lunga S. Barnaba where we turn right into the Campo S. Barnaba. Cinema-goers may recall this as the spot where

Katharine Hepburn fell into the canal in a film called *Midsummer Madness* – and a passer-by, describing the incident to his friends with true Venetian attention to detail, followed suit.

We may now pass on the right of the church of S. Barnaba (there is no need whatever to enter it) and get a new view of the Grand Canal from the S. Samuele *traghetto* stop. There is not very much of interest on the opposite side of the Grand Canal. We see the church and *campo* of S. Samuele and on their left the Palazzo Grassi, once a famous hotel called the Emperor of Austria. Next on the left is the Palazzo Moro-Lin. If we are tired we can go home from here. If it is raining and we feel like a museum, we can do the Ca' Rezzonico (but we must go back and pass round the other side of the church to reach it). It contains a museum of eighteenth-century Venice and gives some impression of what it meant to live in one of the very grandest of the Grand Canal palaces. There are a few fine and interesting pictures, a lot of dull ones, and wonderful views from the windows. The third floor should not be missed, for there the mari-

onettes and apothecary's room are to be seen.

Above all, the Ca' Rezzonico is now the home of the only two view paintings on public exhibition in his native city by Canaletto. One of them shows the same view up the Grand Canal from the Palazzo Balbi as appears on p. 90, but with no Regatta. The other is the view down the Rio dei Mendicanti which we shall come to when we reach Part IV of our second walk on p. 145. Both were painted at the very beginning of Canaletto's career, before he was diverted from large, freely-painted theatrical pictures to the small, sunny topographical views painted to please the English tourist. Venice did well to wait for these magical pictures.

VI. The Frari and its neighbourhood. Whether we continue from our excursion to the Accademia and Zattere or return another day, we are now on the way to the Frari and, finally, to the Rialto Bridge. We start at the Campo S. Barnaba and take the bridge farthest from the Grand Canal of the two crossing the Rio di S. Barnaba. This is the Ponte dei Pugni, one of several bridges used between the thirteenth and seventeenth centuries for fist fights between rival factions of particular pugnacity. They were probably encouraged by the authorities to let off steam in this way as being the least of a nuisance to more peaceful citizens, and bridges without parapets were naturally chosen to add zest to the game. You can still see the four marks of feet set in white stone on the bridge, marking, so to speak, the touch line, but how long these particular marks have been there I cannot say. They look in suspiciously good condition.

Once over the bridge, we follow the Rio Terà Canal, noting that this must be a filled-in canal not because of the word 'Canal'; this was just the name of the family owning the palace on the right. Rio Terà (or Terrà) invariably means a filled-up *rio*, though, and you can generally see where the water used to be. At the end we turn left and so reach the Campo S. Margherita.

We have already left the tourist-beaten ground and are in a typical *campo* where Venetians live and shop. We might do worse than take refreshment here and examine the houses, some of which show easily recognisable traces of their former splendour. Let us walk from the isolated building at the wide end of the *campo* (it was the *scuola* of the fur dressers, a prosperous craft in a city where everybody who could showed off) towards the truncated campanile of S. Margherita. There is no longer any church of S. Margherita. It was closed in 1810 and is now a cultural centre. Before we reach it, though, let us make a curious little digression, certainly not worth noting by the guide books. We turn to the right, down the Calle del Magazen, then left at the end to the Corte dell' Aseo. Someone has built his garden wall through a well-head. The house belonging to the garden, which is numbered 3368, is worth noting for other reasons; it is one of the oldest in the city, old even for Venice.

We go back to the *campo* and turn right to leave it by passing the campanile. High up on the house next to the campanile is a statue of S. Margherita herself; the dragon beneath her is the devil in disguise and it is a relief to know that he devoured her but then burst asunder and vanished, leaving Margherita unhurt. It must have been a nasty moment, though. This came originally from the church and many other relics from it have been embedded in the campanile and the building, which is worth looking at. Just past the cinema-church there will one day again, I hope, be the rare treat of a café by a canal, although sadly it now looks as if it has closed for ever. Anyway, we may pause here where it stood and watch the water traffic, for this is the Rio Nuovo, the short cut to the Grand Canal.

Once over the bridge, we are in the Campo S. Pantalon and we might go to the extreme right of it to examine a slab in the wall regulating the minimum length of the various fish allowed to be sold. We then pass to the right of the church and it is our intention to go to the end of the Calle S. Pantalon and turn left on to the Calle Piovene. The next paragraph is strictly for those with leisure to wander and in a mood for two small digressions.

We turn right into the Campiello Del Angaran where an Angaran has put above his house a figure of an Eastern Emperor. It is certainly a thousand years old. Then at the end of the Calle S. Pantalon we turn *right* and right again down the Calle de la Saoneria to the canal again. At the risk of getting our feet wet, we look across it to the right and see the remains of Byzantine arches bricked up in the wall of that house, number 3368, which we saw in the Corte dell' Aseo. The house was built in the twelfth century, one of only eight such with traceable remains left in Venice according to Ruskin, and the only one not on the Grand Canal. It is by no means one of Venice's grander sights but some of us are moved by it (Ruskin was deeply so). As a result of this digression we have missed the interior of S. Pantalon, the ceiling of which took an artist called Fumiani thirty years to paint and which contains, too, many beautiful pictures of saints. I can but apologise.

We now proceed like sensible tourists and go back, turning left on to the Calle Piovene, and then right at the Calle de la Scuola. We find ourselves at the back of the Scuola S. Rocco and turn left to go right round it, emerging into

the Campo S. Rocco with the front of the Scuola on our right, the church of S. Rocco behind us and the back of the Frari on our left. The front façade of the Scuola S. Rocco looks familiar and it is the scene of Canaletto's fine picture in the National Gallery of *The Doge Visiting the Church and Scuola di S. Rocco*, reproduced opposite. Here is a picture one can stand before for a long time, mingling with the crowds and the Doge's courtiers. It is 16 August, St. Roch's Day, and artists and dealers were allowed on this day to exhibit the pictures they hoped to sell. Canaletto had himself sold a picture here to the Imperial Ambassador some ten years before he painted this masterpiece.

We turn from the scene to the somewhat less attractive figures of the twentieth century about their business in the *campo* and go round past the side entrance of the Frari into the Campo dei Frari. On the right there used to be the premises of a coach-builder who became famous enough to go on building coaches for export long after horses had disappeared from Venice. Often, in eighteenth-century engravings, you will see a

carriage outside his shop and nearly always, as in the one overleaf, some sign of his trade such as wheels and axles. We may be going to visit the Scuola S. Rocco, and even we will pop into the Frari, if only for a few minutes. Refreshment and rest are therefore indicated and, resisting the cafés in the *campo*, we go round to the front of the Frari and over the bridge opposite it to find exactly what we were looking for, a café from which we can contemplate the scene which for Le Corbusier gave 'indeed many a lesson [to town planners] its quayside, its bridge with steps leading over the canal; the little square dominated by the façade of the church, and the main square with its cross and fountain; the campanile and the perspective of the street.'

We must seriously consider going back to the Scuola S. Rocco when we are refreshed and examining its Tintorettos, which made it, in Ruskin's opinion, one of the three most precious buildings in the world – bracketed with the Sistine Chapel and the Campo Santo of Pisa. We may well be asked on our return what we thought of these Tintorettos and it would be

unthinkable to visit Venice without seeing them. Never let it be said that I suggested such a thing. I only point out that the stairs are steep, the pictures, though wonderful, profuse and that they will still be there tomorrow, and, indeed, on our next visit to Venice. But, as compensation for the conscientious, there are some fascinating and highly enjoyable wood carvings by Francesco Pianta with their *trompe l'oeil* library and their caricature of Tintoretto himself.

Before we go into the Frari, we should glance at the building on its right. This is the home of the State Archives, the raw material of a thousand years of history, unmatched anywhere in the world. Rawdon Brown, who spent the greater part of his life in Venice cataloguing the papers which were of interest to scholars of English history, said that there were twelve million volumes of papers in it, all arranged according to the character of their contents. It is not for pleasure seekers like us, but we may reflect that with a small private income and a knowledge of Latin we could spend a happy and rewarding life browsing in this building.

Santa Maria Gloriosa Dei Frari, the Ca' Grande as it was affectionately called, is the sister church to SS. Giovanni e Paolo. Both were built in the fourteenth century, S. Zanipolo, as SS. Giovanni e Paolo is known, for the Dominican friars and this for the Franciscan. There are several ways in which this church can be done. You can, if you wish, find the telephone guide half-way down the left-hand side, insert your money, and wallow in a well-spoken account of the sights at hand. Or you could take your guide book (your real guide book, not this one) and meticulously examine each item after reading a description of it. At the other extreme, you could put the whole thing off until tomorrow, or next visit, or walk to the end and back without looking at anything.

However, we cannot leave Venice without seeing the angels making music in Giovanni Bellini's triptych. This happens to be at the farthest point from the entrance and we shall find much to wonder at on the way. We enter by the main door if it is open, because it is the nearest to our café, and walk down the left-hand side.

First comes the monument Canova designed for Titian but which was eventually used for Canova himself, and serve him right. Next the monument to Doge Giovanni Pesaro who died in 1659, when Venetian baroque was at its most extravagant. 'A huge accumulation of theatrical scenery in marble,' Ruskin called it, the first storey sustained by 'negro caryatides, grinning and horrible . . . on the top of the sarcophagus the full-length statue of the Doge in robes of state stands forward with its arms expanded, like an actor courting applause.' But the Doge is sitting, not standing, and his arms are not expanded. Ruskin's prejudices against the Baroque could distort his vision and if we allow it to distort ours we might well on occasion miss much wit, grace and gaiety.

Titian's tribute to the Pesaro family comes next, recently back from restoration. To Ruskin it was 'the best example of him, by far' in Venice where, as he pointed out, Titian is in general ill represented. No Venetian Renaissance artist achieved Titian's fame outside Venice. The farthest chapel on our left from the main altar has a lovely angel on the monument facing us, perhaps by Donatello, a gloriously framed triptych and a statue of St. John the Baptist by Sansovino. The Milanese chapel next to it has a cruel altarpiece by Alvise Vivarini and Monteverdi's bust above his tomb.

Above the main altar is Titian's *Assumption* which even we must pause to pay our respects to, and, to the right of it, the monument to Francesco Foscari, deposed in 1457 after doing some good and much harm to the State. This can be seen as the last Gothic or the first Renaissance tomb in Venice. In the next chapel is another St. John the Baptist, this time a brightly painted statue by Donatello. And so on to the Sacristy for Giovanni Bellini's triptych in its original sumptuous frame. By the time we have delighted in those angels below the Virgin we can no longer wonder at the Virgin herself. We return to the main body of the church and so into the sunshine, perhaps by way of the side door; if so, we certainly turn to enjoy the newly restored lunette above the door. We have done the Frari.

It is now our intention to find our way to the

Rialto Bridge but first we make a little digression. We cross the bridge in front of the Frari and turn left, passing over another bridge, the Ponte S. Stin. We turn left again and then right. A little farther on, on the left, we find the courtyard of the Scuola di S. Giovanni Evangelista, a piece of Renaissance work which even Ruskin had to admire. It was built by Pietro, the head of that remarkable family of sculptors and architects who came to be known as the Lombardi and who left behind them some of Venice's most precious buildings and works of art. It is in the chapel of this *scuola* that the Cross is housed which was responsible for those miracles we saw being performed in the Accademia.

For today, however, we will content ourselves with the courtyard itself and, having enjoyed it, we return to the Frari the way we came. We pass the café in front of it without this time crossing the bridge leading to the church. Instead we turn left into the Rio Tera, then right on to the Calle Seconda dei Saioneri and keep on following signs pointing to 'Rialto'. We shall soon cross the Ponte S. Polo and reach the Campo S. Polo, for long a great place for bull-fights and tournaments but now a little sad in spite of its fine palaces. In Coryat's day it was 'all greene'. It must have looked gayer when there was a *rio* running in front of the Palazzo Soranzo on the right (its position can be clearly seen); in this palace the young Casanova was one of the hired fiddlers at a three-day ball and helped a sick Senator, who in return adopted him as his son, so making him a nobleman instead of a fiddler.

Still following the signposts along Calle de la Madoneta and then the Calle de Mezo, we reach the Campo S. Aponal and then we are in the Calle de la Rugheta which becomes the Rughetto del Raveno (*ruga* = shopping street). We may notice a timber-beamed shop at the corner of a *calle* called del Paradiso leading off to the right. This will lead to the Riva del Vin by the Grand Canal which is our objective. If we miss it, the next one will do equally well; and if we miss that there are still three more *calli* all leading to the Riva. One of these (Calle de la Madonna) has a well-known restaurant called

Madonna in it. If we miss all these *calli* we shall approach the Rialto Bridge in perhaps the best way of all, via the Ruga degli Orefici (goldsmiths) where we turn right and are in the Campo S. Giacomo di Rialto. S. Giacomo di Rialto, generally called S. Giacometto, is usually given the honour of being Venice's first church – not, of course, this building, early though it is, but its predecessor which was supposed to have been built in 421.

By whichever route we took, we are at the Rialto Bridge and we are on the right side of the Grand Canal to make its acquaintance the first time. Do not cross the bridge, but choose one of the cafés on the Riva del Vin, by the Grand Canal, and settle down. We can now do some sight-seeing in comfort. We are, by the way, just by the site of the palace of the Patriarch of Grado whom we saw curing the lunatic in Carpaccio's *Miracle of the Holy Cross* in the Accademia, reproduced opposite. You can compare Carpaccio's depiction of the old bridge, done in 1494, with de' Barbari's on the right, done about the same time.

VII. The Rialto Bridge to the Piazza S. Marco.

The bridge itself was built at the end of the sixteenth century and there were almost always shops on it. There is an Annunciation carved on its side and the dove, flying towards the Madonna, forms its keystone. It is the Rialto Bridge, not the Rialto. The Rialto (*Rivo alto*, high bank) is the district itself, some say Venice itself, and the two parts of the city connected by the bridge were known variously as *'extra'* (or *'citra'*) *canalem* and *'ultra' canalem*, or as *'di qua dal canale'* and *'di la dal canale'*. Either way, the general meaning was and is 'this side of the canal' or 'that side', 'that' side being the side where we are sitting. It has always been the busiest part of Venice and although the tourists abound they seem to be swallowed up by the Venetians.

Looking across the canal, starting at the bridge itself, we see first a row of undistinguished modern buildings, then, immediately after the small canal, the Palazzo Bembo (Gothic). A little farther down are the Palazzo Loredan, and the Palazzo Farsetti, two Byzantine palaces, or what is left of them, both now the Municipal Offices. After two more palaces comes the huge Palazzo Grimani, now the Court of Appeal, built in the sixteenth century. But instead of reading a catalogue of palace names we would do better to contemplate the scene itself, the very stuff of Venetian life.

Let us take our second cup of coffee on the other side of the Grand Canal but we might, before doing so, read the next page or two in comfort. We shall cross the Bridge on the far (north) side to take in the view looking up the Grand Canal. On the left is the Palace of the Camerlenghi, the City Treasurers; it is a strange five-sided building, of which we can see only part, and already familiar to many of us from Canaletto's paintings of the Rialto Bridge from the north of which it is an inevitable part. The huge building on the right of the Bridge is the Post Office, once the Fondaco dei Tedeschi – a *fondaco* being a warehouse and Tedeschi being Germans. (In Barbari's view it has a caption above it which reads 'Fondaco Alemagna' but I cannot expain the use of this word for 'German' in 1500.) It had been given by the Venetians to the German traders, burnt out and rebuilt by them in the 1500's.

There were several hotels near here (we may remember the sign of The Sturgeon in Carpaccio's *Miracle* in the Accademia) and it was at The Flute, also called The St. George, that Brother Fabri stayed with many other Germans, while waiting for his ship to complete preparations to take them to the Holy Land in 1483. They went first to the Fondaco dei Tedeschi as their headquarters and from there were directed to The Flute. They liked it because the landlord and, indeed, the entire household were German and not a word of Italian was to be heard there. Even the dog jumped with joy as soon as he recognised them for Germans; when Italians, Frenchmen, Greeks or men of any other nationality came near he became so angry you would think he had gone mad. He had not even become accustomed to the Italians living in the neighbourhood or to their dogs – but German dogs were always welcomed. I have been quoting from Brother Fabri's book and he ends by saying that Germans and Italians have a hatred of each other rooted in their nature, that the dog quarrels with Italians because its nature bids it do so but that human beings restrain their feelings by the aid of reason and keep down the feeling of hatred for Italians which is engrained in their nature. No, it is not a misprint: it *was* in 1483 that he was writing.

After the rebuilding the Germans commissioned Giorgione to decorate the Grand Canal façade with frescos of nude figures and Titian to fresco the south side. Canaletto shows faint signs of what remained of the Giorgione frescoes in most of his paintings which include the Grand Canal façade; the Titian fragments seem mostly to have been depicted by his followers. There is certainly not enough to justify the enthusiasm of Ruskin who, a century later, described them as 'flaming like a sunset' when seen from further up the Grand Canal.

And now I must tell a slightly disturbing story of my hero. After Ruskin's death his belongings went to his cousin, Joan Agnew, and her husband, Arthur Severn who sold them over a long period. The final sale, a fairly chaotic one, was in 1931. This included a 'study of a winged cherub', early Italian school, which was bought by Kenneth Clark, perhaps the greatest connoisseur of his day. The experts agree that this is in fact one of the Giorgione frescoes from the Fondaco dei Tedeschi. Yet Ruskin never mentioned it in any of his writings or accounts and there is no record of anyone having seen it in his lifetime. How had he come by it and why the secrecy? Could he just have 'found' the fragment or have been sold it by a workman as rubbish (as it was perhaps regarded at the time)? Nevertheless, however innocently it had been acquired, I wish Ruskin had sent it back to Venice in later life rather than keeping it hidden.

Let us not bother with the names of the other palaces on the right side of the Canal: we have learnt more names than we can remember already today and we shall return to examine them more carefully another day. Let us, instead, look down on the scene with its canal traffic of all kinds and perhaps try to recognise some of them – the *vaporetto*, the *motoscafo*, gondolas, private and public motor-boats, perhaps the dustman's barge, the parcel postman's or the undertaker's, many of them exactly as they looked in Canaletto's day.

Before we descend the steps of the bridge we should cross to the south side. We can see down as far as the Palazzo Foscari. (This is the palace on the corner of the Rio Nuovo leading to the station, the canal in which we saw those Byzantine remains in the wall.) Let us not try to identify anything until we are sitting down; meanwhile we need do no more than enjoy the view, comparable only to that from the Accademia Bridge and, as we get to know Venice better, comprising far more interesting palaces.

We now walk down the Riva del Ferro (Plate 17) and choose a café on its continuation, the Riva del Carbon (where the coal merchants moored their boats). The view is unfortunately interrupted and we may have to get up every now and then to see better. Moreover we cannot go as far down the Riva del Carbon as we should like; if we can summon up courage to go round the back, enter the Court of Appeal at the Ca'

Ponte Rivoalti ad Orientem, usque ad Aedes Foscarorum, cui respondet Ripa Vinaria.

Grimani and talk our way on to the Balcony there, we shall have a better view, but success in this depends on the mood of the guardian and the power of command of the applicant.

There is nothing of special interest on the far side until the Riva del Vin ends, but after that comes a succession of Gothic palaces interspersed with Renaissance ones, each worth studying for its special charm. Remember the scene. Canaletto loved to paint it and the engraving on p. 109 was made after a view he painted from the Rialto Bridge. The Barbari bird's-eye view in the Correr Museum shows this part of the Grand Canal in full sunlight and we can see almost every building as it was in 1500. The palace with the obelisks on the roof is the Coccina-Tiepolo, later called the Papadopoli, a useful landmark; the one before it is the Businello, the next but one after it is the Donà, or Madonetta, both with Byzantine remains – which means that they were private houses 800 years ago.

It is time to go home and we are nearer than you may think. All that is necessary is to walk back to the steps of the Bridge and turn right when we shall find ourselves in the Campo S. Bartolomeo. The campanile of the church is worth remembering as a landmark. The statue of Goldoni, the playwright, smiles down on the busy *campo*. We follow the crowd going to the right off the *campo* and when they divide at the next *campo*, S. Salvatore, we follow those who turn left up Marzaria S. Salvador. We cross only one bridge, the Ponte dei Barretteri (the hat, or beret, makers), an excellent bridge from a scenic point of view. We are now in the Mercerie (plural – each section, in Venetian, a Marzaria) which John Evelyn described in 1645 as 'one of the most delicious streetes in the world' as, in the opinion of many, it still is. When we get to the church of S. Zulian, follow the crowd to the right and then left down the Marzaria de l'Orologio, rather than straight on down the Spadaria. Both routes lead to the Piazza, but the Mercerie route passes under the Clock Tower and, just before we come to it, there used to be a tablet in the paving and a marble relief above it. This is where an old woman lived who achieved fame by chance. She came to her window to see what was going on during a serious rising against the Senate headed by Bajamonte Tiepolo in 1310. Clumsily, she knocked from the sill a heavy marble mortar which fell on to the head of the standard bearer who was riding by below. The insurgents following saw this as an omen of disaster and fled in confusion, and everyone gave Giustina Rossi, for that was her name, the credit for it. Thus did she become a heroine. We are now at the Piazza and may enjoy our aperitif secure in the knowledge that we understand Venice just a little better than we did this morning.

The Riva degli Schiavoni, SS. Giovanni e Paolo, the Rialto Bridge

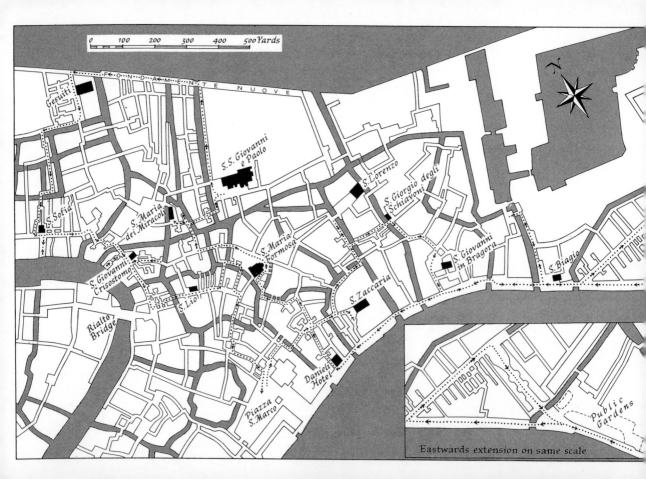

0 100 200 300 400 500 Yards

FONDAMENTE NUOVE

Gesuiti

S. Sofia

S.S. Giovanni e Paolo

S. Maria dei Miracoli

S. Lorenzo

S. Giorgio degli Schiavoni

S. Giovanni Crisostomo

S. Maria Formosa

S. Giovanni in Bragora

S. Biagio

Rialto Bridge

S. Lio

S. Zaccaria

Danieli Hotel

Piazza S. Marco

Public Gardens

Eastwards extension on same scale

WALK 2

The Riva degli Schiavoni,
SS. Giovanni e Paolo, the Rialto Bridge

I. The Scuola di S. Giorgio degli Schiavoni and the Arsenal. The first object of our next walk is to reach a charming café on one of Venice's most attractive canals; the second is to enter another picture gallery. Fear not; it is a very special gallery and has but nine pictures.

We might start at the Piazza as, although our café is very near the Riva degli Schiavoni, it is not easy to reach from there. Besides, there may be some shopping to be done in the Mercerie or a short visit to be paid to St. Mark's. (There is much pleasure to be derived from a series of short visits to St. Mark's; very little from a morning or afternoon devoted to studying its mosaics and other treasures. I know the basilica wasn't

built for giving pleasure but this is a pleasure guide.)

When either has been completed, we leave the Piazza by the Piazzetta dei Leoncini on the north side of St. Mark's. As I have already said, this used to be called the Campo S. Basso after the church closed by Napoleon (but which still stands there. On pp. 116-7 we see it in Bellini's time and Canaletto's). It has not changed much since Canaletto drew it but in the drawing we miss the red marble lions with the inevitable children astride them. They must have been there, though (the lions, not the children), for they took up their position in 1722 and Canaletto certainly drew his picture long after that. The

raised platform on which the well stands, called a *rialto* (which is just a high bank) was to avoid contamination of the water by floods; we shall see many like it in other *campi*. Venetian wells did not reach the water level, which would have been brackish; they were merely collectors of rain water which was filtered through gravel and sand. Before the aqueduct reached Venice there were some 6,000 of them.

Having left the Piazzetta dei Leoncini, at the end of Calle de la Canonica we are confronted by two bridges, but only one leads anywhere, across the Rio di Palazzo behind the Bridge of Sighs. Spare a moment to examine the Renaissance façade of the Doge's Palace from here. Just beyond it we see the point at which the present Palace was begun in about 1300 and at which it was completed (by the Renaissance façade) two hundred years later.

We proceed across the Campo SS. Filippo e Giacomo (*not* turning left off it) and pass, with some difficulty, a shop full of particularly appetising Venetian fried specialities, arriving at the Ponte S. Provolo which crosses the second *rio*

off the Riva degli Schiavoni, the Rio del Vin. Across the bridge, we are confronted by a gateway with a marble relief above it which leads to the church of S. Zaccaria. We might pass through the gate into the unusual *campo* and the church of S. Zaccaria, which looks so familiar as a result of all the Venetian Renaissance copies which became fashionable in England in the nineteenth century; it might almost be the home of a millionaire in Park Lane. We might even enter the church and find, on our left near the entrance, Giovanni Bellini's *Virgin with Four Saints*. This was one of the treasures stolen by Napoleon and it was kept in Paris for twenty years during which time it was transferred from panel to canvas. Nowhere but in Paris could this have been done at the time and it probably saved the picture for posterity.

On the other hand, we might turn left at the gateway leading to S. Zaccaria and postpone our visit to it, proceeding instead across the Campo S. Provolo to the Fondamenta del Osmarin (rosemary), a delectable little *fondamenta* with the Palazzo Priuli (fine windows) on the left. It leads straight to our objective, the Rio S. Lorenzo with its café with a few seats alongside the canal where we may take coffee, an ice-cream or even lunch if it happens to be lunch time. On the other side of the *rio*, towards the lagoon, is the church of S. Giorgio dei Greci, the Greeks' own church, with its leaning campanile; it started to lean as soon as it was built in 1592 and has always been a source of anxiety.

If, before we sit down, we walk up the rio, along the Fondamenta S. Lorenzo, with the reproduction overleaf in front of us, we shall have no difficulty in finding the spot at which Gentile Bellini stood to paint his *Miracle of the Holy Cross* 500 years ago. It is no good looking for the Cross; divine intervention made it float so that it could be picked up easily. Otherwise, everything is much as it was then. The palaces along the banks of the canal are all splendid but just the former homes of rich Venetian citizens of no particular distinction.

Now let us consider, at our leisure, the pictures we are going to see in the Scuola di S. Giorgio degli Schiavoni, for that is where we are going. I know we have already done the Accademia and the Frari and that we did not come to Venice to look at pictures but I think you will find this worthwhile.

The *scuola* was the guildhall of the Dalmatians (Slavs) who ran it, among other purposes, as a kind of seamen's institute for the benefit of visiting Dalmatians. Coryat pointed out to his readers three hundred years ago that the Venetian *scuole* were not designed for merriments and banquetings as the halls belonging to the Livery Companies of London were, but rather for devotion and religion. Both went in for good works, though (the London Companies still do, together with the merriments and banquetings), and the Dalmatians, who had done well out of their trading in Venice, commissioned Carpaccio to decorate their hall for them. Carpaccio had already done his St. Ursula series for another *scuola* and was near the peak of his career; had they been able to find a Dalmatian artist of equal rank they would have preferred it, but none was to be found. Carpaccio, fortunately,

was willing to use Dalmatian saints for his subjects, so the contract was signed.

It is often said that here we see paintings in the place for which they were designed, but this is not so. They were designed for an upper hall and moved down to their present position when the building was entirely rebuilt fifty years later, in 1552. Neither are they in their original order, but they look comfortable where they have been for some four hundred years, even though we may not have the same impression on entering the *scuola* as Ruskin – 'a little room about the size of the commercial parlour of an old-fashioned English inn; perhaps an inch or two higher in the ceiling . . .'

There are nine paintings, three about St. George, three (I insist, but authority says two) about St. Jerome, one about St. Tryphonius; a *Christ in the Garden of Gethsemane* and a *Call of St. Matthew*.

St. George first, then. He was not, as some of us think, an Englishman, although Edward III made him our patron saint. So little is known about who he was, indeed, that the Church decided he should be placed among those saints whose names are justly revered among men, but whose actions are known only to God. As far as the Dalmatians were concerned, he was a Dalmatian and, when he was on his knightly travels in Libya, he came into a city where a monstrous dragon was causing much trouble by breathing its poisonous breath over everyone and everything. They tried to placate the monster, first with sheep, then with children and finally with the king's own daughter, Princess Cleodolinda, who had been chosen by lot as the dragon's next victim. George, who had not yet been sainted, of course, found her walking towards the dragon's swamp and, when it appeared, he made the sign of the cross at which the dragon submitted to his spear. This we see in the first picture and, from the remains of the dragon's earlier meals scattered in the foreground, we can imagine what the poor princess was spared. In the second picture, George, about to cut off the dragon's head, is enjoying his triumph, and in the third he is receiving his reward. The king had offered all his gold and half his kingdom for his daughter's redemption, but George asked only that they should be converted to Christianity and here we see him baptising them himself. Dreadful things were to happen to George later on, resulting in sanctification from which, alas, he was demoted in 1969. Here, all is happiness, though, so we pass on to St. Tryphonius.

St. Tryphonius does not appear in my book of saints and there is little about him in the booklet which the *scuola* sells (with the usual quaint translation but unusually well-reproduced photographs). He was a Dalmatian boy who had a gift for casting out devils (like the Patriarch of Grado whom Carpaccio had already depicted performing a similar miracle by the Rialto Bridge for the Scuola S. Giovanni Evangelista which we saw in the Accademia). It was the daughter of the Emperor of Rome whom the devil had chosen to possess on this occasion and Tryphonius was sent for. Knowing his reputation, the devil, complaining bitterly, promptly left the princess on hearing the news of his approach. When Tryphonius arrived, the Emperor insisted

that the devil should be called back to explain his conduct and this Tryphonius encompassed, persuading him moreover to confess all his wicked works and so lead to more conversions to Christianity. Carpaccio's picture represents the argument between the boy and the devil (depicted as a basilisk, a winged devil with a cock's head in heraldry), leading to the confession. It is generally called *St. Tryphonius subduing the Basilisk* with no justification whatever; we do not know what became of the devil, but he was not 'subdued'.

The next two pictures are scenes from the Bible, the first, *Christ in the Garden*, of little interest, but the second, the *Call of St. Matthew*, of much. We see the publican leaving a Venetian money-changer's stall to follow his Master. The background could only be a town in the Veneto on the mainland; the publican's counting house behind his stall is full of fascinating bric-à-brac.

Finally, three pictures of St. Jerome, everybody's favourite saint and, in this case, accepted by all as a Dalmatian. Nobody wanted to hurt Jerome and he never hurt anybody, not even in the cause of Christianity. He was rich enough to retire young and he went to Bethlehem where he founded a monastery. There a lion came to him with a thorn in his foot and stayed to protect his benefactor when the thorn had been removed. Jerome's fellow monks do not seem to have much confidence in his powers over the lion in the first picture, and in the second they do not even seem to have allowed the lion to attend his beloved master's funeral (it must have been that stern one with the spectacles on his nose reading the service who forbade it).

The third and last picture is the celebrated *St. Jerome in his Study*. There is not a detail of this picture to be missed, from the little white dog in the foreground (it was to have been a cat, as we know from a preliminary drawing now in the British Museum) to the altar and cupboard and books and music – everything will conspire to keep you out of the fresh air. Perhaps the best thing is to imbibe the colours, remember as much as possible, but leave the picture long before you have done with it and buy a reproduction to take home for the cold winter evenings.

The cause of Truth compels me to refer briefly to the fact that there is a movement on foot to call this picture *The Vision of St. Augustine* instead of what everybody knows it to be, *St. Jerome in his Study*. Such arguments are used as that the mitre in the foreground must belong to a bishop and St. Jerome never was a bishop; also (a little more plausibly, I fear) that the lion is absent and St. Jerome would not have had a dog in his study. Nevertheless, I pass over this new attempt by art historians to deprive us of our most cherished traditions with the contempt it deserves.

Let us get up. We cross the Rio S. Lorenzo by the brick bridge, that is to say the one between the Ponte S. Lorenzo and the one at the point where we entered the *fondamenta*. Keeping left (important) on to the Calle Lion we cross another canal, the Rio della Pietà, and are outside the Scuola di S. Giorgio degli Schiavoni.

When we come out we follow the Fondamenta dei Furlani left along the canal as far as we can then turn left again along the Salizada S. Antonino. To the right at its end (but easy to miss) is a *campo* called Bandiera e Moro, Venetian noblemen who gave their lives for United Italy as early as 1844. They foolishly wrote of their plans to England; the Government caused their letters to be opened and reported the contents to their enemies. This *campo* had a rare distinction in that it was at one time called '*Piazza Bandiera e Moro*'. As everyone knows, there is really only one *piazza*, the Piazza S. Marco, and this one was stripped of this title early this century, becoming a *campo* like all the other *campi*. There is a palace in the *campo* called the Gritti Badoer (No. 3608, now a well-known pensione called La Residenza) which Ruskin considered 'a magnificent example of the fourteenth century Gothic, circa 1310', that is, before the Doge's Palace. He added a sad note to a later edition of *The Stones of Venice*: 'The building is now a ruin, inhabited by the lowest orders; the first floor by a laundress,' and, in 1877, a terser and sadder one, 'Restored and destroyed.' Ruskin was always at his most vituperative over restoration but never very clear about the alternative to it. The church of S. Giovanni in Bragora is known for a Cima da Conegliano

Baptism of Christ over the altar – a beauty, but too far away to see easily. We leave the *campo* by the opposite corner along the Calle del Dose, which will take us out on to the Riva degli Schiavoni where we turn left, cross a bridge and reach the Arsenale *vaporetto* stop. If we look back we shall see the majestic view Canaletto painted (Plate 18 and opposite the Preface to the Eighth Edition) which is now in Sir John Soane's Museum; and we could compare Whistler's speedy etching opposite. Whistler, called the Artful Doger of Venice by one reviewer, was staying at a pensione here, and this view is what he saw from his room.

The long, low building in the right foreground of Canaletto's picture was the Forni Militari, the military bakeries, and had already been so for several centuries. We may now turn left up the Calle dei Forni if we intend to visit the Arsenal, and we should really pay a brief visit at any rate to the strange agglomeration of buildings which form the entrance. It was, after all, from this spot that the source of all Venice's wealth came, for, without her fleet, she would have

been nothing. Tourists have always been taken to see the Arsenal, although they were shown only what it was considered good for them to see. It was here that the conveyor belt system was devised and the ships, when completed, were towed past the windows of the storehouses, ten at a time, stores and equipment being added at each point until, by the time they reached the end of the dock, they were ready to sail. Important visitors were shown a keel in the morning and, by evening, it had become a complete seaworthy galley. On one occasion, for the benefit of Henry III of France, the whole operation was completed while 3,000 guests were banqueting. A Spanish pilgrim described it all in the sixteenth century.

The triumphal arch was the first Renaissance building in Venice (1460) and the gods and goddesses were put in front of it in the seventeenth century to commemorate one of Venice's few victories of that period. The two outside lions came about the same time and have always aroused interest, particularly the one on the left. He came from Athens, where he was much loved,

in spite of Ruskin's view that he was 'stupid work of the Greek decadence, mere cumber of ground'. To everyone's surprise, the inscription on him turned out, quite recently, to be in old Scandinavian, put there in the eleventh century by a Norwegian soldier fighting in the Mediterranean.

We cross the wooden bridge and make our way back to the Riva along the Fondamenta de l'Arsenal. Here we turn left by the church of S. Biagio and the Naval Museum, which will be irresistible to lovers of ships and naval warfare but easily resisted by others. It is full of guns, boats and a few (surprisingly few) interesting maps. We proceed along the Riva and after crossing another bridge we branch away from it along a wide and busy street (in fact, the widest in Venice) created by filling up a canal. It was called Via Eugenia after Eugène de Beauharnais, Napoleon's stepson and viceroy who was really responsible for everything done in Venice in the name of Napoleon. Now it has become the Via Garibaldi and the picture opposite shows it as it was after the cholera had broken out in

1849 and brought final doom to Manin's Republic. We can still see where the canal ran, and when it was filled in the street became the route to the new Public Gardens; it remained the only route until the beginning of this century when the Riva was extended and that extension now provides the usual way of reaching them. We are following the old way, though, and when we see the gardens open out on the right we enter them and soon find ourselves back on the Riva.

A little farther along, on our left, is the entrance to the Biennale, the International Exhibition of Modern Art. If the year happens to be an odd numbered one we shall have a difficult decision, whether to enter it or not. If it is an even numbered year, there is no problem; there is no Biennale so we enter the Paradiso Restaurant instead. Modest though its culinary aspirations may be, it has a hypnotic view which interests some of us more than modern art.

II. View from the Public Gardens. From our table at the Paradiso we can contemplate the City and its southern suburbs as they stand today – always bearing in mind that the first arrivals at Venice looked out on to a different scene and that it will be a little different even tomorrow. The lagoon is always changing whatever efforts the Magistracy of the Waters, as the responsible department has been called for six hundred years, makes to keep it as it is. Thus the island of Malamocco, the original capital of Venice, no longer exists; it was swallowed up by the waters eight hundred years ago. The rivers brought down silt; islands were formed; they became inhabited; the mud rose; the islands became uninhabitable. So it went on and, although the rivers now take most of their silt out into the Adriatic, so to some extent it will always go on.

The original Malamocco was off the island we call The Lido, one of the two long narrow tracts of land between the peninsula which stretches off the mainland from the north and Chioggia in the south. It is The Lido which we see on our left stretching away into the background. The other island is now called Pellestrina but originally they were both called *lidi*, or beaches, together with the other narrow islands which formed the outer shell of the lagoon and which have now become part of the mainland. Malamocco is now a fishing village on the Lido but farther down than the *vaporetto* stop to which we see so much traffic heading. That is S. Maria Elisabetta and the modern temple which provides a landmark we shall become very familiar with is S. Maria della Vittoria. The interesting end of the Lido is the end near us for it is here that the old church of S. Nicolo stands, here where Byron rode and Ruskin walked, and where the two old burial grounds of the Protestants and the Jews may be found 'neither of whom are allowed to rest in consecrated ground', explained Goethe. He had just, at last, seen the sea with his own eyes 'and walked upon the beautiful threshing floor of the sand which it leaves behind when it ebbs'. Byron, to return to him, not only rode but swam on this part of the Lido and on one occasion swam a race against an Italian and another Englishman starting at S. Nicolo and finishing, in Byron's case, at the far end of the Grand Canal. The Italian had dropped out early and

the Englishman could get only as far as the Rialto Bridge.

At the extreme end, too far to the left for us to be able to see it, is the great Porto di Lido, by far the most important of the three *porti*, to and from which we can probably see ships of all sizes passing. The other *porti* are the Porto di Malamocco, between the islands of Lido and Pellestrina, and the Porto di Chioggia, between Pellestrina and Chioggia. There were others but they have been lost since Nature seems to be for ever struggling to seal off the lagoon from the Adriatic and so stifle Venice until she sinks into the mud like the other islands. So long as the Porto di Lido can be kept open, Venice can survive and at one time there was even talk of letting Malamocco and Chioggia go the way of the others; Malamocco has been kept as an insurance, though, and so has Chioggia although neither is used by the big ships.

In front of the Lido, and all the way round to the right of our scene, stretches a group of islands. In the centre is the sand dune, variable in size according to the state of the tide, which separates the Canale S. Marco in front of us from the Canale Orfano on the far side of the sand. We can see six islands to the left of the sandbank of which two are hospitals, Le Isole del Dolore, the Islands of Sorrow. The nearest is S. Servolo on the extreme left, originally a monastery, then an asylum for what the Serenissima described as 'noble maniacs', then and still a mental home. Then comes S. Lazzaro, the only one of this group we are likely to visit. We may want to be shown round the island by the Armenian monks who will gladly display their printing press, their museum and every spot which Byron hallowed while amusing himself with a light-hearted study of the Armenian language. Behind S. Lazzaro is Lazaretto Vecchio, once a prosperous island, since 1965 abandoned, and then to the right S. Clemente, Sacca Sessola and La Grazia, respectively another mental home, a chest hospital and a women's hospital. All these hospital islands can be visited from one *vaporetto* called 'Ospedale', run for the benefit of relatives and officials of the hospitals, but not even S. Clemente, with its

huge buildings and Baroque church, has anything to offer tourists like us.

To the right of the sandbank we see the island of S. Giorgio Maggiore and, peeping behind its left or western end, the western tip of the Giudecca island – the tip with Cipriani's Hotel on it. To the right of S. Giorgio Maggiore is the Salute and the entrance to the Grand Canal, and on our right we can see all the way along the Riva degli Schiavoni and up the Grand Canal as far as the roof of the Palazzo Corner della Ca' Grande, Sansovino's huge Renaissance palace, now the Prefecture. The only building which stands out between us and the Doge's Palace is the church of the Pietà, about half-way, built in the eighteenth century except for the façade; this never got further than the bases and lower parts of the columns, as we can see from many post-1750 paintings, but in 1906 the money was found to finish it according to the original plan.

If, when we leave the Paradiso, we care to walk to the end of the Viale Trieste (which is what the Riva degli Schiavoni has changed its

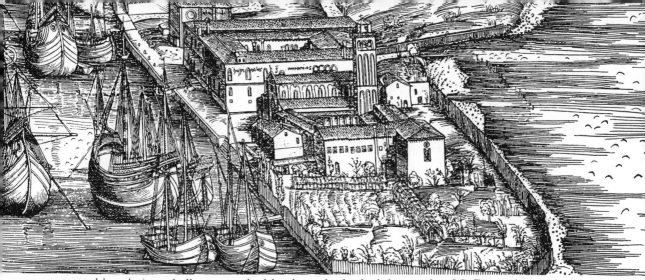

name to at this point) we shall come to the island of S. Elena, but there is little enough to draw us to this quarter. It was once the loneliest part of Venice and its easternmost point. Now, almost entirely on reclaimed land, a populous area of modern flats has been built. The reclaiming of land has always been a Venetian speciality and by the time Barbari drew his view there had just been an important undertaking of this kind completed in this neighbourhood. The Senate had asked the monks of S. Domenico to give up part of their garden, partly to enlarge the neighbouring monastery of S. Antonio but also because they wanted more space to foster the pilgrim trade. The monks refused, to the fury of the Doge and Senate (three hundred years later Napoleon did rough justice to all by abolishing Doge, Senate and then both monasteries to provide space for his Public Gardens) so there was nothing for it but to reclaim land from the

sea. The Senate did not like important people staying in hotels; they preferred to take over palaces or put up new ones to house them. It was customary to provide all important visitors with their food at public expense, wherever they were staying, and the Senate showed their disapproval of those who insisted on staying in inns by sending up small and scurvy meals to them. Those who accepted public hospitality, on the other hand, were liberally fed, and some of the buildings shown in the Barbari view were used for this purpose. We cannot help wondering what was behind this attitude of the Senate. They claimed it was unbecoming for one bound on so holy a pilgrimage to stay in an inn but there must have been more to it than that. Some of the pilgrims were men of influence and knowledge in their own countries. Had the Venetians introduced the 'bugging' of visitors' rooms as well as so much else?

The detail from the Barbari view on p. 131 shows this part of the city; opposite is an aerial view taken from the angle Barbari imagined himself to be – it should be compared with the whole view reproduced on pp. 10-11. The detail below is from a map drawn in Canaletto's time.

There was then no land to the east of the drawing except a small part of the island of S. Pietro, the remainder of which is seen in the top right-hand part of the view. Now, as can be seen from the photograph, there is the whole man-made island of S. Elena. Even more reclamation has taken place on the western side of the city to enable the dockyard area and the Piazzale Roma to be built – together with the new artificial island car park. It was here in the east, though, that it started.

If we really feel like wandering in this part of the city, we could make our way north and reach another island, that of S. Pietro, connected by

two bridges to Venice itself. Here we should be standing in front of St. Mark's predecessor as the Cathedral of Venice, for that was the proud title borne by S. Pietro until 1807. There are better things to devote our energies to, however, and we should retrace our steps by the *Riva*, named in turn, after Viale Trieste, the Riva dei Sette Martiri (martyrs, not of the Risorgimento in this case, but of the Second World War during which they were shot by the Germans), Riva S. Biagio, Riva della Ca' di Dio and finally Riva degli Schiavoni.

III. The Riva degli Schiavoni to SS. Giovanni e Paolo.

We are now on ground we know and just before we reach the Danieli Hotel we might pause at one of the last cafés on the Riva, choose a table by the edge of the water and ponder the question of whether to continue our expedition or go back to our hotel and return here another day. Our plan is to travel north and there is much to see, so, unless we feel fresh, postponement might well be indicated. If, on the other hand, it is lunch time we could not do better than go to Malamocco in the Calle del Vin just before the bridge.

We are going to leave the Riva by one of the two *calli* between which the new Danieli Hotel stands but, before doing so, we pause and consider the buildings (Plate 20). The Prison was built about the same time as the present Rialto Bridge and by the same architect, Antonio da Ponte. This was almost a hundred years after Barbari had drawn his bird's-eye view in the Correr Museum, which I so often refer to and which is dated 1500. The prison has always exerted a macabre fascination over visitors, particularly since Casanova's escape from it. They still quail at the fresh looking names and lamentations carved by the prisoners of the past on their cell walls. But in 1833, Bulwer Lytton's wife Rosina wrote home that 'the guide told us they were nearly effaced till Lord Byron had spent two days re-cutting them into the walls.' By Barbari's time the Palazzo Dandolo, which is now the Danieli Hotel proper, was a hundred-year-old building and it appears in his view much as it is now. It became a hotel in 1822 but has always been used to accommodate illustrious visitors to Venice; even as a hotel it has always been 'the best in Venice' as Murray described it in 1846, and Ruskin stayed here many times before and after his four-month sojourn in 1849-50 to prepare for the first volume of *The Stones of Venice*. (It was so cold for part of the time that he and his wife played Battledore and Shuttlecock in the hall to keep warm.)

The Danieli Hotel management provide no memento of the work Ruskin did there in Room 32 but in Room 10 it is recorded that George Sand and Alfred de Musset were past occupants. They were indeed, but their failure to find what the hotel's brochure calls 'their dream of absolute, true and complete love' was hardly due, as the management complains, to their having been 'trop exigeant' as clients. The truth was that de Musset told his mistress on their first night there that he did not love her and proceeded on a course of debauchery in the Venetian slums, while George Sand seduced a young doctor called Pagello whom she later took to Paris before discarding him (he returned to

Venice, married and lived happily ever after, or at any rate until he was ninety-one).

Between the original hotel and the Prison there remained for at least two hundred years – and no doubt before that – a commonplace group of huts and buildings made memorable only by the fact that, occupying the position they did, they necessarily found their way into innumerable paintings, drawings and photographs of the Riva degli Schiavoni at this point. (See overleaf for an early photograph and a Canaletto from an unusual viewpoint.) It is an astonishing fact that they were allowed to remain where they were for so long (they were 'about to be destroyed to make room for an addition to Hotel Danieli' in Major Douglas's time, forty years before the event took place), but it may be that any architect was daunted by the prospect of designing a building to stand in such a position. There was, moreover, a technical problem to overcome, a very Venetian one. In 1102 a Doge Vitale Michiel I was murdered here and his assassin took refuge in one of the houses. He was found and hanged but the risk

of such a thing happening again could not be contemplated. Orders were therefore given that the houses be destroyed and never again rebuilt in stone. For eight hundred years, therefore, only low wooden houses were permitted here and the proprietors of the Danieli Hotel had not only to find the right architect, but also to persuade the authorities that they were not endangering the life of the community by permitting a new building to go up here. Eventually, however in the late 1940's, a sufficiently dauntless architect was found and before we criticise his work too harshly let us ask ourselves whether we could have done better. Would we have preferred a fake Gothic or neo-Renaissance structure, of which Venice already has so many? Should the site have been declared beyond the capacity of any architect and turned into a garden? Or should the old huts and dwellings have been allowed to remain where they were until they acquired the picturesqueness of a ruin? We must think charitably of the dilemma confronting the architect of the Danieli Royal Excelsior Hotel, as it describes itself in an effort to get the best of all possible worlds, and turn our back on his work to contemplate the Riva at this point.

Before the Riva was built the houses were lapped by the waters of the lagoon but there has been a paved embankment for over six hundred years. Until 1782 though, it was only the width of the bridges as they then were, and that is how Canaletto painted it (p. 137). A white marble strip let into the paving shows its extent.

We can now go up the Calle dei Albanesi (the one next to the Prison), or the Calle delle Rasse. This was where they sold the *Rassa*, which was a thick black fabric from Serbia used for roofing the *felze* (cabins) of gondolas; nearly all the gondolas we see in old pictures were closed in. We duly arrive at the Campo SS. Filippo e Giacomo which we passed on our way to the Rio S. Lorenzo. This time we continue straight across. We take the second turning to the left into the Campo S. Giovanni in Oleo at a sign reading 'Galleria Querini Stampalia' and then turn right under a *sottoportico* to a *fondamenta* and so to the Campiello Querini Stampalia. In this

Gallery you may learn much of how eighteenth-century Venetians spent their time from an unrivalled collection of genre pictures by Pietro Longhi and Gabriele Bella. There is much else to see in this elegant house – and you are now allowed to go around on your own, a recent and much appreciated amenity.

Once we have left this *campiello* we reach the Campo S. Maria Formosa (Plate 21). This *campo* is one of the city's best known and best loved, familiarised by drawings and paintings of its vigorous life, its market, its open-air theatre, its bull-fights and the palaces which surround it. They have the usual names and the usual histories but the design of each is full of individuality. Readers of *The Stones of Venice*, if they still exist, will find on the western side of the campanile, facing the canal, the grotesque mask Ruskin made so much fuss about ('A head, – huge, inhuman, and monstrous, leering in bestial degradation, too foul to be either pictured or described, or to be beheld for more than an instant.') It forms the keystone of the arch. If we are weary there is a café with tables on the *fondamenta* behind the church which we might like to inspect.

We leave the *campo* by the *calle* farthest away from the church, called de Borgoloco, and cross two bridges. We then take care to turn right at the near side of Campo S. Marina and reach a splendid view from the Ponte del Cristo. After a long pause, we proceed along the Fondamenta Van Axel, at the end of which is the Palazzo Van Axel (although it is also known as the Palazzo Soranzo or Venier or Barozzi). Its wooden door, with its strange knocker, is irresistible to the photographer and has been so since photography was invented. At the end of the *fondamenta* we turn left into the Calle Castelli and we are outside S. Maria dei Miracoli, by no means an easy church to find if approached from the more usual direction. This little Renaissance church is a miracle indeed and should be entered even by the pleasure seeker, indeed especially by him. Even Ruskin noted it as one of the most important buildings in Italy although he was grudging enough in admiring its sculptures as 'the best possible examples of bad style'. He couldn't bear the child's head tied up by the hair at the base of the right-hand pilaster at the top of the altar steps. 'The man who could carve a child's head so perfectly must have been wanting in all human feeling,' he wrote, 'to cut it off and tie it by the hair to a vine leaf.' If you want to know all about the church, another Lombardo master-piece, there is a telephone guide at your disposal. And remember that it was completed before Richard III died at Bosworth.

We return to the Palazzo Van Axel, catch a glimpse of a lovely garden, and cross the canal on which the palace stands instead of going back the way we came. The bridge, the Ponte de le Erbe, soon leads to another bridge from which the scene looks familiar. It is the point from which Bellotto (if it was Bellotto, and not Canaletto, or both together) painted his *Scuola Grande di San Marco* which we saw in the Accad-emia (reproduced opposite). We have entered the easternmost sestiere of Castello, as a sign points out to us, and, just as we hoped, there are several cafés awaiting us round the corner. We first glance up the canal to the open lagoon at the end and the cemetery island of S. Michele beyond it and then settle ourselves down.

We are in the Campo SS. Giovanni e Paolo and facing us is Verrochio's statue of Bartolomeo Colleoni on his horse. It is here for a curious reason. It was paid for by Colleoni himself, who left enough money for a really splendid eques-trian statue provided it was erected in the Piazza S. Marco. Andrea Verrochio, whom one associ-ates only with Florence, but who spent the last eight years of his life in Venice, was commis-sioned to make the statue and had practically finished it when he died in 1488. He must have been having trouble over the casting for a long time, for, already in 1483, Brother Fabri was writing 'as for what will be done about casting it I have not heard; perhaps they will give the whole matter up'. Five years later, with his death, the problem had become acute and the only sculptor thought able to solve the problem was Alessandro Leopardi, who had designed the bronze bases for the three standards in front of St. Mark's. Leopardi was a true Venetian, unlike Verrochio, but he had unhappily been convicted

of fraud the year before and exiled from Venice. He was recalled and carried out the casting and finishing successfully for which he was rewarded by having his name, and not Verrochio's, engraved on the statue, under the horse's band. Colleoni's condition that his statue was to stand in the Piazza S. Marco raised no difficulty. The idea of putting any statue in such a position was preposterous, so the Venetians told themselves that the Scuola S. Marco was practically the same thing. It would be nice to be able to say that the campo was at that time called S. Marco, but its name has always been as it is now. We need not trouble ourselves too much, however, about the consciences of the Venetian Signoria, who had anyway been guilty of graver chicanery than this in their time. Nor need we worry too much about Colleoni, the victim of the deception. He was as efficient a general as anyone could wish for but his services were available to anyone prepared to pay his price and it is doubtful if he would ever have been heard of again if he had not had the good fortune to be the subject of what is often called the greatest equestrian statue in the world – and, until 1866, the *only* outdoor public monument to anyone in all Venice. (The one rival for the title of greatest equestrian statue is Donatello's statue of Gattamelata in Padua, curiously enough, another *condottiere*, or mercenary captain. It was a great thing to be in Italy in the days of the Renaissance if money and power were what you wanted. Colleoni on his death-bed warned Venice never to give another general the power she had given him. 'I could have done you much harm,' he added ominously.)

The *scuola* itself replaced the S. Marco fraternity's first building which was burnt down after only twelve years. It was started in 1485 and its façade has a curious charm, easy though it is to criticize it (Plate 22). The building has been the city's principal hospital since the beginning of the nineteenth century and extends all the way back to the lagoon. Ruskin bracketed it with the Miracoli as 'the two most refined buildings in Venice' in what he called the Byzantine Renaissance style. The Lombardo family, again.

The church of SS. Giovanni e Paolo is collo- quially called S. Zanipolo, a less far-fetched corruption than others such as S. Trovaso for SS. Gervasio e Protasio, or S. Marcuola for SS. Ermagora e Fortunato. With the Frari, it forms Venice's great pair of Gothic churches, and the great names of Venice resound as one examines its tombs and monuments.

If we really are in Venice to examine tombs and monuments, this is the place. And very moving many of them are, especially some of the early ones in and around the apse. The baroque monument to the Valiers on the right wall would shock those of us who had not seen the Pesaro tomb in the Frari. To reach it we pass Giovanni Bellini's early (1460's) polyptych with a painful St. Sebastian and an enchanting predella. Past the Valiers, still on the right, there is a happy *trompe l'oeil* picture by Lorenzo Lotto of St. Anthony and beyond that the great Gothic window, perhaps still invisible owing to restora- tions. But for the British 'Venice in Peril' fund it would not have remained visible at all for long, but probably be in pieces on the floor or in the street. A very Venetian touch to the church is provided by the walls. These, of course, are of brick but natural bricks would scarcely do for the last resting place of so many honoured servants of the Republic. The walls have therefore been plastered over to enable artists to paint a suitable background – and what background was regarded as the most suitable to paint? Bricks. A small clue to the Venetian mind, but a clue. There is much to be learned about Venice in SS. Giovanni e Paolo if we do decide to go inside.

On the other hand, we may decide to postpone the expedition – or it may be lunch-time and the church closed anyway. In either happy event, we walk along the Fondamenta dei Mendicanti beside the hospital (Plate 23) and pass a *squero*, or boatyard (now a rare sight and becoming rarer) which was certainly there in Canaletto's time. This was the *rio* used by Casanova to reach the Palazzo Bragadin, his best friend's house in Venice and the scene of many of his exploits, from his *casino* in Murano which he used as a country cottage. We emerge at the Fondamente Nuove (the new embankments) which were built

in 1589. We are on Venice's north shore, although, as we can see from the Barbari view on p. 148, both the Scuola S. Marco and SS. Giovanni e Paolo were beside the water until the Fondamente Nuove were built.

IV. View from the Fondamente Nuove.
We turn around and there is the view down the Rio dei Mendicanti which Canaletto painted in his early picture now in the Ca' Rezzonico. To our right is the campanile of S. Francesco della Vigna. The *fondamenta* does not reach the church; it ends a short distance from where we are, for by then we get close to the Arsenal and the preservation of the secrets of the Arsenal was, until quite recently, a matter of prime concern to the Venetian authorities. Long after the time when there could have been no secrets left to conceal, it was clear from maps that cartographers, like everyone else, were forbidden to enter. It is closed to this day, except for occasional Biennale events; even the *vaporetto* that used to speed excitingly through it has been rerouted. The boat used to leave from the spot where Canaletto painted the little picture opposite; the blank walls to the left are the Arsenal, and the campanile is that of S. Francesco.

S. Francesco has a huge, rather dull façade by Palladio, some Doges' tombs and a fine Negroponte which is difficult to see. We shall do better to turn left, away from it, cross two bridges, pass a number of flower shops (we are near a cemetery) and settle down at a café – say, perhaps the one just before the next bridge.

It is from here that the *motoscafi* leave for the cemetery island of S. Michele and Murano, also for Burano and Torcello. We could go from here to Treporti, too, if we wanted to; we should then be on the mainland since Treporti is on the peninsula which, with the islands of Lido and Pellestrina, forms the outer shell of the lagoon. There is something to be said for avoiding the Piazzale Roma by driving to Treporti and Punta Sabbioni, which is at the very end of the peninsula, parking one's car there, and taking a *vaporetto* to the Riva degli Schiavoni. There is indeed something to be said for any stratagem to avoid the Piazzale Roma and its satellite island, Tronchetto, which, despite its capacity for 7,000 cars, is sometimes full. There are overflow car parks at S. Giuliano and Fusina, the traditional point of entry to Venice for centuries, but it is better to arrive by air, rail or water than by road.

We are unable to see the islands of Burano and Torcello from where we are sitting, but S. Michele with its cypresses and brick wall and Murano on its left are very close.

The cemetery at S. Michele is another of Napoleon's innovations although some sort of cemetery would inevitably have been needed even had he never appeared; the campi round the churches must have been getting very full of dead Venetians by that time. The island was therefore turned into a cemetery, but already by 1837 it was getting so crowded that the adjoining island of S. Cristoforo was added to it. Good use was thus made of at least two of the islands of the lagoon, which is more than can be said for the fate of most of them. Some are used for hospitals but a number were taken over by the military and no less than ten of these have been abandoned in the last twenty years. Their future is in the balance, as indeed is the question of whether they have a future at all.

How the lagoon looked before Napoleon's improvements we can see in Francesco Guardi's painting on Plate 25. It is a clear day; the water is full of boats, and the islands full of campaniles. A few hundred years earlier Brother Fabri rowed out to S. Cristoforo one day while waiting for his boat to take him to the Holy Land. He wanted to beg S. Cristoforo to bear him safely across the seas, also to provide him with good and honourable inns – 'or, at all events, provide us with patience to bear the shortcomings of our inns during our long journey'. No wonder St. Christopher is the patron saint of the Travel Agents' Association.

We ourselves are unlikely to visit S. Michele, as it is now called, unless there is a Protestant grave we have some wish to find. Only Protestants remain there for more than ten years and then only if they have bought themselves space in the little Protestant cemetery adjoining the main Catholic one. All others are allowed ten years of rest and then get transplanted to the public ossuary or, if their relatives pay the price, to a rather higher class ossuary. Until quite recently their journey was a longer one for the bones were taken to the island of S. Arianna on the north of the lagoon where they were piled up.

If we came in from the airport by the Alilaguna we saw something of Murano and we must return there. Ruskin would be displeased if we missed the church of S. Donato altogether after he had devoted twenty-five pages of his *Stones* to a description of it. Even he, though, warned his reader that he was in for a hard day's work, so we had better postpone the plan. The glass museum, too, now has something to offer (see p. 208).

Ruskin loved to come to this part of Venice, to walk along the *fondamenta* and look at the hundred-and-fifty-mile stretch of Alps; this was in the winter, though, and in summer, more often than not, only the foothills of the Alps are visible, if those. It was here that the Venetians built their smaller palaces, away from the pomp of the Grand Canal, and their gardens ran down to the waters of the lagoon. Titian had one, very close to where we are sitting, and one of his visitors has described how, before dinner, they sat in the garden looking across to Murano, the water swarming with gondolas 'adorned with beautiful women and resounding with varied harmonies'. When the *fondamenta* was built the houses lost their view and privacy and the district became a slum as it still is. The detail from the Barbari view overleaf shows clearly how it was and the map on p. 114 shows what it has become today.

V. Between the Fondamente Nuove and the Rialto Bridge.

We could, if we wished, turn left by the side of our café next to the Ponte Dona and go down the Calle delle Tres Crose to see the site of Titian's house. It is really not worth while, though, just a tablet set in the wall of a dingy block of flats, so, when we have finished our coffee, we cross the high bridge, continue along the *fondamenta*, and turn left down the Salizada dei Spechieri

On our left is the church of the Gesuiti, the

altar end of which would be in the lagoon by now but for the action of one of the American restoration funds. Nineteenth-century guide-book writers found it inexpressibly vulgar but taste changes and we may well find its interior witty and entertaining – although entertainment may not have been the object of Domenico Rossi, who designed the pulpit with its glorious damask curtains which turn out on examination to be made of marble, like almost everything else in the church. It was the Manin family who provided the money for this greatest of all Venetian show-offs and we might shed a sympathetic tear for the universally execrated Ludovic Manin, the last Doge of all, the one who ended the thousand-year glory of the Serenissima by handing it over to Napoleon. What else could he have done in the circumstances?

We return to the sunlight and reason and turn left outside the church into its *campo*. This was a great place for *scuole*, the cask makers, tailors, silk weavers and gold-lace makers all having their guildhalls here, and many having their sites still marked by tablets in the walls. There is also the oratory of the Crociferi restored by a group of private organizations – one of them is Venice in Peril – which makes an enjoyable short diversion with its cycle of paintings by Palma Giovane.

If it is lunch time we could now cross the *rio* and arrive at Da Nino, a modest trattoria, or, if feeling self-indulgent, continue in a southerly direction (i.e., away from the Lagoon) to Vecia Cavana, favourite Venetian restaurant of that celebrated gourmet, Mr Bernard Levin, in the Rio Terrà Franceschi. Otherwise we turn right off the Campo dei Gesuiti, pass the three Zen palaces, once frescoed by Tintoretto on the outside, and cross the next bridge on the left, the Ponte S. Caterina. When we can go no further we turn right under the wooden eaves of a much photographed palace, left over the Ponte Priuli and so along the Calle Priuli to the Strada Nova.

We shall get to know this street very well and should mark the spot at which we have entered it. If we were to turn to the right instead of the left, we should reach the station, the street having changed its name on the way to the Rio Terrà di Maddalena and Rio Terrà S. Leonardo and finally to Lista di Spagna. We thus know that part of the street was made by filling in canals and indeed it was almost certainly the first street in Venice so to be made. We are turning to the left, however, and all we have to do to reach the Rialto Bridge is to follow the crowd. This part of the street came much later, not until 1872, and was, not unexpectedly, named Via Vittorio Emanuele. There was no canal to be filled in here, just houses to be knocked down, and it is interesting to follow the course of the entire street and notice the difference between those parts which have always had houses lining them, albeit once by the side of a canal, and those which have fairly recently been built. The street will change its name several times while we walk along it.

Before we follow the crowd to the Rialto Bridge, we glance at the church of S. Sofia on our left which has had the misfortune to lose its façade behind houses, above which it pops up rather surprisingly. Opposite the church is its *campo*, from which there is a *traghetto* we shall later patronize. Meanwhile, the *campo* is worth entering for it is well kept by the gondoliers and there is a view across the Grand Canal. Standing at the edge of the *campo* we see on the extreme left the Campanile of St. Mark's, one which we already know well; this will reassure us that we are not as far from home as we may have thought. The nearer campanile is S. Bartolomeo's, one which it is well to memorise as it appears from many unexpected points and can be helpful to bewildered travellers longing for a familiar landmark. Beware of it, though, for the campanile of SS. Apostoli is hard to distinguish from it; SS. Apostoli has stone columns at the top whereas S. Bartolomeo has brick ones.

On the opposite side of the canal we see the fish and vegetable markets and to their right a series of palaces of which the two most prominent are eighteenth-century ones, of imposing proportions, the first being the Palazzo Corner della Regina, the Monte di Pietà or Municipal Pawnshop, and a few doors farther up, the Palazzo Pesaro, now the Museum of Modern Art (not *very* modern: for that you must go to Mrs

Guggenheim's at the Palazzo Venier).

Now we really do start our walk down the Strada Nova and soon reach the Campo SS. Apostoli where we turn right over the bridge. We pass under the palace of the notorious Doge Marin Falier who lost his head in 1356 and who is represented by an empty canvas in the Doge's Palace, alone in disgrace, surrounded by portraits of his illustrious predecessors and successors. We follow the crowd for a few minutes and come to another church, S. Giovanni Crisostomo. It contains Giovanni Bellini's last painting over the altar 'among the most perfect in the world', according to Ruskin, and a famous Sebastiano del Piombo of S. Giovanni Crisostomo himself. It will probably be closed: no matter. Either after visiting the church or instead of doing so, we look for an unpromising alley to the right just before the church, perhaps still marked Calle del Scaleter o de la Stua, and find our way through it to a delectable little courtyard on the Grand Canal. It is called Campiello del Remer and Ruskin delighted in the remains of Byzantine capitals and arches which may be seen above the

outside stairway. We are lucky to see them for in 1540 the owner of the palace, Maffeo Lion, gave away the Serenissima's secrets to the French; he was banished and his palace ordered to be destroyed. Lion had apparently foreseen the possibility, and, like others before and after him, showed he had made half of it over to his wife and in any case the other half belonged to his brother. Thus the palace and its courtyard were saved for Ruskin and ourselves to enjoy. We get an unusually good view from here of the Rialto Bridge and the Palace of the Camerlenghi and of the campanile of S. Bartolomeo.

Again we return to our Strada Nova, now the Salizada S. Giovanni Crisostomo. We must have left the newly-built part of the street for Salizada indicates the principal street of a parish, indeed very often, until towards the end of the eighteenth century, the only paved one. On our left we may notice a sign pointing to Da Nane Mora, a good restaurant with a pleasant garden, well worth a visit another time if not now. Even if we are not patronizing the restaurant, though, we should make a little diversion here by passing to the right of it to the Corte Seconda del Milione, named after Marco Polo's book of travels written in the thirteenth century. Around us are remains of some extremely old palaces, and in Ruskin's words 'fragments of the old building in every direction, cornices, windows, and doors, of almost every period, mingled among modern rebuilding and restoration of all degrees of dignity'. There is a Byzantine arch on the left which intrigued him greatly: his friend Rawdon Brown wrote, between Ruskin's two principal visits to Venice, calling it a 'horseshoe' arch but Ruskin demanded measurements as he was convinced its shape was due only to pressure from above. He had left Venice only a few weeks previously and was to return the following year but he could hardly contain his impatience to see the arch again for himself. Curiously enough, he does not include this building among his eight houses with Byzantine remains.

Ruskin called the house with the arch Marco Polo's but it is not now considered so to be. For this we must pass under another *sottoportico* to the Rio dei Miracoli and the Ponte Marco Polo. On

the left we shall then see a building with a tablet let into its wall saying that this was where Marco Polo's house stood. It subsequently became a theatre which closed in the nineteenth century after some two centuries.

Now we return to the Salizada S. Giovanni Crisostomo and follow the crowd over the Ponte de l'Ogio (*ogio* – oil in Venetian). We are leaving the Sestiere of Canareggio and entering that of S. Marco and there on the wall is a sign showing the ultimate number in the S. Marco sestiere – 5562. The crowd now leads us to the Campo S. Bartolomeo, presided over by the smiling statue of Carlo Goldoni, Venice's leading playwright, and now our street has become the Via 2 Aprile. This was the day in 1849 when Venice proclaimed resistance against the Austrians 'at all costs'.

We are back to the Rialto Bridge area (there it is on the right) where the Venetians swamp the tourists, and, so as to keep away from them ourselves a little longer, we will not follow the crowd, which will take us down the Mercerie, but will turn left off the *campo* under the Sotto-

Plate 17: We now walk down the Riva del Ferro (p. 108).
Looking up the Riva del Ferro from the wigmaker's shop

Plate 18 (preceding pages and Frontispiece): We shall now see the majestic view Canaletto painted which is now in Sir John Soane's museum (p. 124)

Plates 19 & 20: We are going to leave the Riva but before doing so we pause to consider the buildings (p. 134)

Plate 21: This campo *is one of the city's best known and best loved: Campo S. Maria Formosa (p. 139)*

Plate 22: We are here in the Campo SS. Giovanni e Paolo (p. 140)

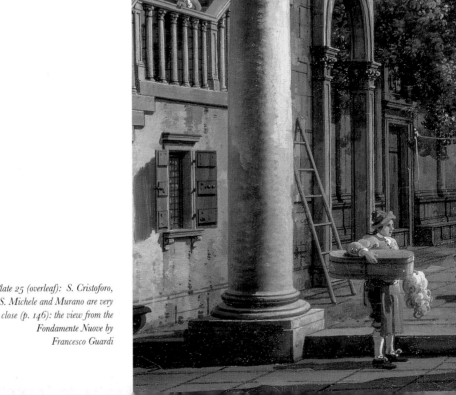

Plates 23 & 24: A capriccio by Canaletto based on the view of the Scuola S. Marco from the campo opposite (p. 143)

Plate 25 (overleaf): S. Cristoforo, S. Michele and Murano are very close (p. 146): the view from the Fondamente Nuove by Francesco Guardi

Plate 26: There are some fine palaces surrounding the Campo S. Angelo and we get a good view of the leaning campanile of S. Stefano (p. 163)

Plate 27: The huge Vendramin Calergi Palace (right) . . . up the Grand Canal we see S. Geremia (p. 191)

Plate 28: S. Simeone Piccolo (left), the architect must have had the Pantheon in mind (p. 205)

Plate 29: S. Lucia and the other buildings demolished and supplanted by the railway station (p. 205). The Scalzi, right, is still standing

portego de la Bissa and cross the Ponte S. Antonio (*Bissa* is adder and the *calle* certainly winds about like one). We pause on the bridge which is over an important canal, the Rio della Fava. It joins the Grand Canal just above the Rialto Bridge; if we followed it on our right it would become the Rio della Guerra which we are going to cross in a moment, and then the Rio Palazzo, coming out under the Bridge of Sighs.

We come next to the Campo S. Lio and if we want to see the Ponte del Pistor, which was Turner's favourite, we must turn left. It is scarcely worth the digression, though, so we pass to the right of the church along the Salizada S. Lio. Canaletto lived and died in the Corte della Malvasia for which we would have to turn right after the church and go through the Corte Perini. If we are making for home, though, we go straight on, looking out for a *calle* on the left, the Calle del Paradiso. We do turn down this, for at its end is an attractive bridge on which innumerable artists and photographers have stood to record the arch connecting the houses of the Foscari and the Mocenigos. We can see a door built to lead down to the canal which, if the tide is high, is practically submerged; it is a sad sight and we proceed over the Ponte del Paradiso, turn right, and here we are at the Campo S. Maria Formosa again. We go only a few yards and turn right before entering the campo, to cross the canal again by the Ponte del Mondo Novo. At the end of the *calle* we turn left and right into the Calle delle Bande, which leads us across the Rio della Guerra, by one of the bridges formerly without parapets used for fighting between rival sects, and so to the back of the Campo S. Zulian, turning left down the Spadaria which runs parallel with the Mercerie, and the Calle Larga S. Marco. The area abounds with restaurants, some of which, such as the Do Forni, Al Conte Pescaor and the Città di Milano try harder than others. Do not expect them to be cheap if you order expensive dishes and remember that you can reach Harry's Bar in five minutes if you are not in an experimental mood.

WALK 3

The Sestiere di S. Marco

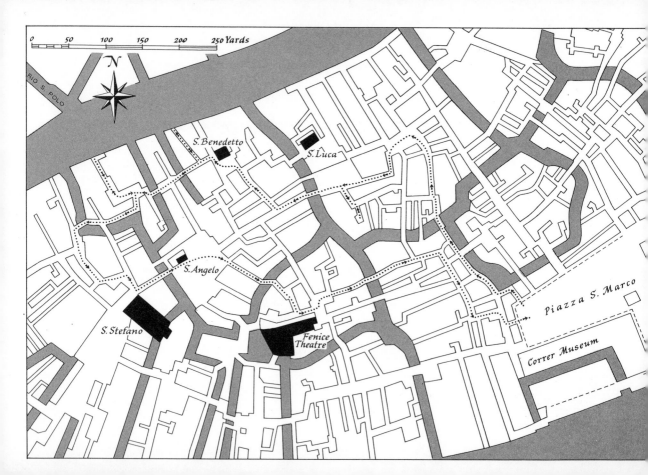

0 50 100 150 200 250 Yards

N

RIO S. POLO

S. Benedetto

S. Lûca

S. Angelo

S. Stefano

Fenice
Theatre

Piazza S. Marco

Correr Museum

The Sestiere di S. Marco

I. The Sestiere di S. Marco. After some quite long walks, it is time for an easy day and we propose to examine that tongue of land formed by the loop of the Grand Canal between the Rialto Bridge and the Salute. It is in the *sestiere* (section) of S. Marco and we should note that there are, and have been for seven hundred years, six sestieri, three on the near (that is, the east and north) side of the Grand Canal and three on the far side. S. Marco is the central *sestiere*; Castello, in which the Arsenal lies, the eastern and largest. Canareggio is the northern one and is divided by long parallel canals of which the largest and most important is the Canareggio itself.

Across the Grand Canal there is Dorsoduro ('Hardback') which is all the southern part including the island of Giudecca; then S. Polo,

the central part which includes the Frari, and, finally, S. Croce, named after a non-existent church and including the Piazzale Roma; it used to include Murano, but that was changed in 1271. The postal address of a Venetian is the name of the *sestiere* in which he lives followed by a number. The numbers are consecutive in the truest sense, that is to say number 2 is next door to number 1 even though it be in a street leading off number 1's street. The numbers go down the *calli*, round the *corti* and back up the other side of the *calli* so that two houses facing one another across the corners of a street will have very different numbers. If your friend has a palace on the Zattere, you do not address your envelope to him at his palace followed by 'Zattere'; you put 'Dorsoduro, 1234' or whatever the number is. Nevertheless, I see quite a number of envelopes addressed in the more comprehensible manner and they always seem to arrive. The system results in numbers going above 5,000 in the sestiere of S. Marco and to 6,420 in Canareggio. Do not despair. You can always wait for the postman if you really need to know where a house is and know nothing but its number.

In addition to the six *sestieri*, the city is divided into thirty quite small parishes, nearly all named after churches we gradually get to know. Both *sestiere* and *parrochia* are clearly shown at many points and are helpful in fixing our position; street names are well marked, too, although often in the Venetian vernacular which seems strange at first sight – and second sight, too, until one gets used to it.

And so to the parishes of S. Luca, S. Stefano and S. Maria del Giglio in the *sestiere* of S. Marco. We have already walked through the southern part on our way to the Accademia Bridge so today we leave the Piazza by the farthest *calle* away from St. Mark's off the Procuratie Vecchie – the north-west tip of the Piazza. This leads us at once to the Bacino Orseolo,

the nearest point to the Piazza which one can reach by gondola; it was built only in 1869 so one can imagine the congestion when there was nothing here but a narrow canal. We follow the crowd in a northerly direction and inevitably find ourselves in the busy Campo S. Luca, traditionally the centre of Venice. We turn left and make for the Campo Manin, from which we will make two short, but worthwhile diversions.

First we turn right down a *calle* on the near (northern) edge of the *campo*, and into the Campiello de la Chiesa. Here, opposite the church, is a very early Gothic door which captivated Ruskin with its eight types of brick. Now back, and so again into the Campo Manin, formerly the Campo S. Paternian but now named after the leader of the 1848 rising against the Austrians of which we shall see much in the Correr Risorgimento Museum which we hope to visit later today. He lived in the house at the end of the *campo* between the two bridges and we saw the place where his ashes rest in the Piazzetta dei Leoncini.

Next we leave the *campo* by a small *calle* on the

south side, opposite his statue, turn left at the end of it and then right and reach the back of the Palazzo Contarini del Bovolo with its famous spiral staircase, which we can inspect through the bars which surround it. (*Bovolo* is Venetian for 'spiral'; you will not find it in the dictionary.) The front of this Gothic palace is on the Rio di S. Luca and we shall be able to see it later. Meanwhile, we return the way we came, along the Calle della Vida (wine) o delle Locande (or of the inns: there used to be at least three) and back to the Campo Manin where we turn left, cross the Ponte della Cortesia and take the first turning to the right, the Salizada della Chiesa o del Teatro. We reach the Campo S. Benedetto dominated by the fourteenth-century Palazzo Pesaro which is now a museum full of works by Mariano Fortuny, including those incredible pleated dresses our grandmothers wore. We follow the Calle del Traghetto on the left of the Palace for a new glimpse of the Grand Canal.

It is unfortunate that there is no café here for there is much for us to see. Let us therefore find somewhere to make ourselves as comfortable as possible and note, first, on our right that we can see the campanile of S. Bartolomeo by the Rialto Bridge. The stretch of the Grand Canal facing us is the part which is in full sunlight in Barbari's view of 1500, see overleaf; it is the only part on which the sun shines in his drawing that we can still see, for the northern stretch has been altered beyond recognition by the station and Piazzale Roma buildings. We may need a little imagination to link the palaces we can see with those Barbari saw and, of course, many of them were built since his day. With his marvellous view in our minds, though, and a determination not to be too critical, we may have an enjoyable few minutes.

Immediately opposite us are the two Palazzi Dona, with the traghetto station between them. The one on the left was called by Ruskin the Madonetta House, after a relief of the Madonna and Child in the façade, and the other he called the Braided House, after the pattern on the capitals of the central windows. In his diary he called the Braided House 'Police House' and it was indeed then the office of the *Questura*. These

were two of the eight palaces with Byzantine traces left in his time, and, if we look towards the right up the Grand Canal, we shall see two more. Before we reach them, though, we see the Palazzo Coccina Tiepolo immediately to the right of the Palazzo Dona, a landmark because of its obelisks (the other palace with obelisks, the Palazzo Balbi, can just be seen right down the Grand Canal to the left; we will remember that it is next to the Ca' Foscari with the Rio Nuovo in between). The Palazzo Coccina Tiepolo is just opposite the Palazzo Grimani, on our side of the Grand Canal, which, James Morris tells us, was built by a suitor for the hand of a young Coccina Tiepolo. To impress his future father-in-law in true Venetian style he made all the principal windows of the Grimani Palace bigger than the main portal of the Coccina Tiepolo. You will sometimes find this palace called Papadopoli after the family who owned it in the last century and who gave the Papadopoli Gardens, by the station, to Venice.

The next palace to the right is the Businello, a seventeenth-century palace 'lately restored' in Ruskin's time but bearing Byzantine mouldings. He writes, of the restorations, 'without his being implicated in the shame of them, they fitted this palace to become the residence of the kindest friend I had in Venice'. This was Rawdon Brown whom we recalled when we were at the door of the State Archives by the Frari, where he spent most of his life. Taglioni, the dancer, owned the Businello while Rawdon Brown lived there. Perhaps she was the culprit?

Next to the Businello is the Rampinelli and then the Barzizza of which Ruskin said, 'Half of the house is visibly modern, and there is a great seam, like the edge of a scar, between it and the ancient remnant, in which the circular bands of the Byzantine arches will be instantly recognized.' I cannot claim to have instantly recognized the remains of the Byzantine arches; if you would like to try you should go to the S. Silvestro *vaporetto* stop just to the right of it.

We have, by the way, almost completed our collection of the eight Byzantine palaces. Two of them, the Farsetti and Loredan, we saw from the Riva del Vin on the other side of the Rialto

Bridge and then passed when we crossed to this side. One of them was the cause of that ridiculous digression which prevented us from studying the ceiling of S. Pantalon – you remember we wanted to see the canal frontage of that house with its garden wall through a well-head. One of them was the Fondaco dei Turchi, far up the Grand Canal beyond the Rialto Bridge. The remaining four stand opposite us. No one will ever ask us whether we saw Ruskin's eight Byzantine palaces but perhaps we can visualize 'that first and fairest Venice which rose out of the barrenness of the lagoon; a city of graceful arcades and gleaming walls, veined with azure and warm with gold, and fretted with marble'.

We now look at the palaces to the left of the Dona and come first to the Palazzo Bernardo. It was built in 1442 and has been altered less than most so it must have looked much the same when Barbari drew his view of it with the sunshine pouring in. No effort of imagination is needed to recognize it in the detail from the view on p. 160. The wide canal leading into the Grand Canal just right of centre in the Barbari

view is the Rio S. Polo and the campanile whose steeple can be seen to the right of that, on our side of the Grand Canal, is marked S. Beneto (S. Benedetto) which is just behind where we are standing. And where else in the world, pray, can you sit with a 500-year-old drawing in your hands and pick out one building after another on it still standing? The palace to the left of the Bernardo is the seventeenth-century Querini-Dubois, then another Grimani palace, but originally built by the Giustinians in the sixteenth century; then the Capello palace by the side of the Rio S. Polo. Sir Henry Layard, the archaeologist, lived and kept his paintings here, most of which are now in the National Gallery, London.

Let us return to the Campo S. Benedetto. Turn to the right off it up the Calle Pesaro and over the Ponte Michiel and Ponte de l'Albero. Then turn right through the Corte de l'Albero to the S. Angelo *vaporetto* stop and its little *fondamenta*. The Palazzo della Terrazza Barbarigo with its enviable terrace is now opposite us; in the last century it was famous for its pictures, including seventeen Titians, all of which are now in the Hermitage collection at St Petersburg. The splendid Gothic Pisani Moretta comes next, another palace we can easily identify in Barbari's view (it was built in 1420). The Palazzo Barbarigo della Terrazza is not there as it had not yet been built but we can see the space it was to occupy. Then come two Tiepolo palaces followed by a succession of less interesting ones down as far as the Palazzo Balbi. We must leave the Grand Canal and proceed on our way. Our close examination of one stretch of it from one point will have given us a better understanding of its character than any number of trips up and down it picking out the high spots.

We return to the Corte de l'Albero and, when we can, turn right off it down the Ramo Narisi to the little Fondamenta Narisi. Looking from here down the canal which runs away from us we see the campanile of S. Stefano and, in the distance, the Salute. Travelling as nearly straight ahead as we can, we reach the Piscina S. Samuele (a *piscina* is always the site of a former pond) and proceed along it. At the end of it, on the left, there are some steps leading up to a pleasant and unusual raised courtyard, called Campiello Nuovo o dei Morti. We are in reality standing over a disused cemetery (*Morti* – the dead), filled in after the plague of 1630 and covered over; not until two hundred years later was it considered safe to let the public walk over it. Down the steps at the other side, turn right and we are between the *campi* of S. Stefano on our right and S. Angelo on our left. We know S. Stefano (but if the church is open and we have not yet been in, it is worth entering to see the marble work on the altar) so we turn left to the Campo S. Angelo (Plate 26). Just as we enter it, on the right, is the entrance to the cloister of S. Stefano. It is entirely occupied by Government offices but, if it is open, it is worth going in and looking round.

There are some fine palaces surrounding the Campo S. Angelo and we get a good view of the leaning campanile of S. Stefano. There is nothing else so, unless we want to patronize one of the cafés at the far end of the *campo*, we turn right at that end into the Calle de Cafetier below some curious curved brick buttresses. At the bridge there is a glimpse, to the right, of the water entrance of the Fenice Theatre, the only entrance which anyone who was anyone thought of using, until quite recently. The Ruskins, for example, were living at what is now the Gritti Hotel, an easy five minutes' walk from the theatre, but it never seems to have occurred to them to walk except one night when they lost their gondolier. The congestion must have been barely tolerable, whereas today one's gondola could park right outside for the whole evening without complaint; everyone walks.

We pass under a *sottoportico* and find, on our left, a small building to commemorate the resistance of April 1849, with a portrait of Daniele Manin and a collection of cannon balls fired by the Austrians against the Venetians and collected after the bombardment. Turning left, we reach the Campo S. Fantin, the front entrance of the Fenice Theatre and, on the right, the Antico Martini restaurant, which has been called the best restaurant in the city.

The Fenice (Phoenix) Theatre did indeed rise from the ashes only six months after a disastrous fire in 1836, and has now done so again after another in 1996, but, curiously enough, it was already called the Fenice when originally built in 1791. From the day it opened it has always been Venice's principal theatre although then one of many. It has had its great days as, for instance, the first night of Verdi's *La Traviata*, and it was always the meeting place of Venetian society. Sometimes this aspect went too far and Effie Ruskin complained that it was impossible to pay any attention to the opera as callers kept coming to her box 'making it a sort of Babel'. Everyone was against her, though; 'they said that the Theatre was public property and everybody had a right to call on anybody that they knew, and as most people went every night for an hour it was economical as it saved them lighting their rooms at home, and that having a box at the Opera was the cheapest way for all to see people and society.'

The theatre used to be owned and operated by its box holders, descendants of the noble families who had originally built it. A box, then, was an asset of high value but eventually it became a liability and after the First World War the holders were glad to hand both their privileges and responsibilities over to the municipality. Whether its performances be dismal or brilliant, and they can be either today, the theatre itself is surely the prettiest in all Europe, and every effort must be made to get inside before leaving Venice. It is not only the auditorium which delights, but also the banqueting and retiring rooms. All the more remarkable that all this beauty is the result of the most painstaking restoration, for there was little enough left of the original after the last fire. Everything, including the supreme Royal Box, can now be seen on a guided tour.

But this is not for today, so we pass the theatre's dull exterior, pass the church of S. Fantin on the left – now a centre of scholarship, the Ateneo Veneto – and reach the Ponte dei Barcaroli o del Cuoridoro. From here, on the left, we see the façade of the Palazzo Contarini del Bovolo, whose spiral staircase we saw earlier, and, on the right, a tablet marking the stay in Venice of the fifteen-year-old Mozart in 1771. It is our last bridge, for at the end of the *calle* we turn right into the Frezzeria. To the right off this street a *calle* leads to the Piscina de Frezzaria and the restaurant La Colomba, with a well-known collection of menu covers on the theme of its name, the dove. We turn left into the Bocca di Piazza and are soon at the entrance to the Correr Museum. We must now consider a few notes on this excellent museum and also on another Venetian institution.

II. The Correr Museum. As we passed through the Frezzeria, we might have observed a flashily dressed lady with a marked interest in unaccompanied gentlemen (they must be elsewhere than the Frezzeria but that is where they seem most abundant). Like so many Venetians, she has a noble lineage. Venice has always been accommodating to her tourists, be they crusaders, pilgrims or protégés of American Express, and one of the accommodations many tourists expect is the availability of courtesans. The City was regulating them as long ago as 1443 and one particularly successful one is said to have built an Augustinian monastery. Coryat was entranced by them, although a little shocked by their numbers – at least 20,000 whose quivers were open to every arrow. He expressed proper disgust at the dispensation granted to the profession by the authorities, but explained in its defence that it did help to preserve the chastity of Venetian wives – and, of all the indignities in the world the Venetian cannot patiently endure, he went on, the worst is that he should be capricornified, or cuckolded.

But their contribution was greater than this. The revenues they paid the State maintained a dozen of its galleys and their fame drew men to Venice from the remotest parts of Christendom. Their palaces were glorious and glittering to behold; they wore chains of gold and orient pearl over their damask gowns laced with brocade; they would enchant you (or, at any rate, Coryat) with melodious notes on the lute or a rhetorical discourse, according to your taste. But woe betide you if you tried to escape without paying; they were, after all, Venetian. He tells us all about their lives, even to the bringing up of their children, but, he ends, they have but few: according to the old proverb, 'the best carpenters make the fewest chips'.

Now let us consider the Correr Museum. It is, in fact, only part of the Correr Museum that we are to visit, other parts of the collection being spread over the Ca' Rezzonico which has all the eighteenth-century part, the island of Murano which has its glass collection, Goldoni's house which has become a museum and the Ca' Pesaro which is the modern art gallery. The collection was started by Teodoro Correr whose family had all the right associations. They were, for instance, noblemen before 1297 after which date new families were admitted to the Great Council and the standing of a nobleman was never quite the same. One of the family was sister to a Pope, and mother and grandmother to two more Popes, and the family were still recorded in the Golden Book when Napoleon entered Venice in 1797. This book held the names of all members of the Great Council and by this time there were 1,218 names recorded.

Teodoro gave his collection to the City in 1830 and it continued to grow, being housed in the 'restored' Fondaco dei Turchi (see p. 188) at the end of the last century. Meanwhile, the splendid palace which Napoleon had made of the Procuratie Nuove and his own new wing at the end of the Piazza had in turn become the palace of the Emperors of Austria and the Kings of Italy. This is the palace which, after the First World War, became the main home of the Correr Museum and which we are about to enter.

Lovers of sculpture and painting will find plenty to enjoy here (including Carpaccio's *The Courtesans*, now more happily called *Two Venetian Noblewomen*, which Ruskin called 'the best picture in the world,' adding as an afterthought, 'putting aside higher conditions and looking only to perfection of execution'). Those who love Venice, as did Teodoro Correr himself, will find furniture, documents, robes, portraits and much that exists nowhere else. Map lovers will hurry through to Room 14 where a great treasure awaits them – no less than the actual wooden blocks cut by Jacopo de' Barbari from which

his bird's-eye view we are already so familiar with was printed. If you study it closely you may almost have the illusion of wandering along the mediaeval streets, albeit in reverse so that you have to turn left when you should turn right. There is also, as would be expected, a fine impression of the engraving itself – look for instance, at the Danieli Hotel in which every window pane appears in a space less than 1½ inches wide (p. 203).

In the same room there is a fine collection of maps and views, in which we see, growing before our eyes, the city of Venice, more land ever being reclaimed from the sea.

Either now or on a later visit we should see the Risorgimento Museum which is next to the picture gallery on the second floor. Here we are nearer our own times and find ourselves among people wearing our sort of clothes and thinking our sort of thoughts. The many mementos of those who endured so much for the freedom they considered worth any sacrifice are indeed moving, and the watercolour and tempera drawings of Luigi Querena and others give us an incomparable feeling of the atmosphere of Venice during the 1848 rising. This is the date we think of in connection with the Venetian Risorgimento, or rising, but the exhibition reminds us that the Venetians have been resisting at various times from 1797, when the Treaty of Campoformio gave their city to the French, up to 1945 when the Germans were in occupation. We could even say 'till 1997', when some insurrectionists 'liberated' the Campanile on the 200th anniversary of the fall of the Republic.

In Room 4 we may notice a painting of the scene when Manin addressed the crowds in the Piazza from a window in the Procuratie Nuove and called upon them to resist at all costs. On the way out we may pause at the very window and see the Piazza exactly as Manin looked out upon it. Only the purposefulness of the crowds thronging it has changed.

WALK 4

The Grand Canal and the Canareggio area

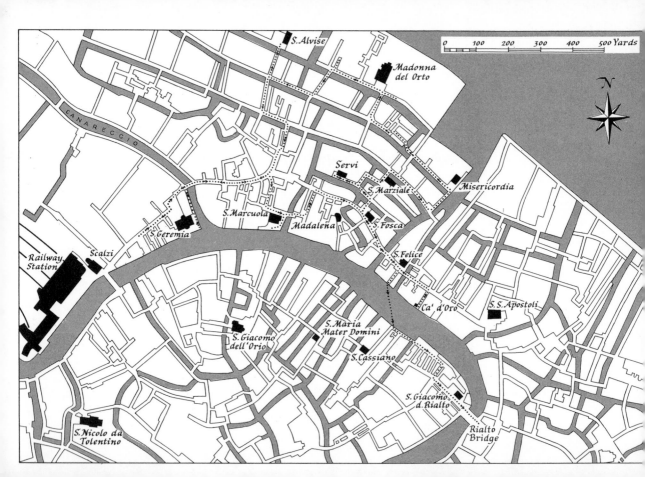

The Grand Canal
and the Canareggio area

I. The Ca' d'Oro. If anyone asks us whether we have been inside the Doge's Palace we can reply 'not yet, but we have seen almost every building on the Grand Canal, as far up as the Rialto Bridge, from dry land,' and this is something that few tourists – and fewer still Venetians – can boast. Today, let us refresh our memory of them by starting our expedition with a *vaporetto* trip up the Grand Canal. Let us first turn that 'almost' into 'quite' by booking to S. Tomà on the No. 1. At S. Tomà we disembark for a look across the Grand Canal at a part we have hitherto missed.

Looking back down the Grand Canal on our own side we can see as far as the Ca' Rezzonico stop which we visited briefly on our way to the Frari. We see the Rezzonico, the two Giustinian and the Foscari palaces, the last on the far side of the Rio di Foscari which farther up becomes the Rio Nuovo. On the near side of the Rio Foscari is the Palazzo Balbi, and we saw those on our left, including the Pisani Moretta, from the S. Angelo stop which we remember going to just for its view.

It is, therefore, only the palaces opposite us which we have not seen and they consist primarily of four great houses grouped together, originally forming the Mocenigo palaces. The one immediately opposite us was the oldest, indeed the courtyard side of it, which we cannot see, is Gothic. The Grand Canal façade, though, was built in the seventeenth century to match the palace at the other end which had been built some hundred years earlier. Later on, the two outside ones were connected by the two inside ones, all really one great house but now all separately owned. An English diplomat, Lord Arundel, lived here in 1622 and one Antonio Foscarini was strangled by the Republic who could not believe he could be visiting the English milord for any but treasonable reasons. In fact, as was discovered a year later, it was love of Lady Arundel that drove him there, but it was too late by then.

It is Byron, though, whose name will always be associated with the palace, more even, perhaps, than the Mocenigos themselves, for all their seven Doges. He came in 1818, the wife of the draper in the Frezzeria having been supplanted in his affections by the baker's wife, the Fornarina, as he called her. There were tumultuous scenes at the palace between Byron and his past and present mistresses, culminating in the Fornarina marching in on Byron and a friend at dinner and seizing a knife from the table. She was conducted downstairs while dinner proceeded but soon had to be fished out of the Grand Canal and 'refixed' from her wetting, and the salt water she had swallowed, by a surgeon sent for by Byron. Finally, she was dismissed for ever and Byron turned his attentions to the Countess Guiccioli, a liaison that was to prove more serious and long lasting.

It was here, in the same year, that Shelley arrived on a poignant mission. He had brought Byron's discarded mistress, Clare Clairmont, to Venice to see her child, referred to by Byron in his correspondence as 'it' or 'my bastard', then staying with the British Consul after a few months at the Mocenigo palace with her father. Perhaps she was better off there for at the Mocenigo palace, apart from the tempestuous Fornarina, there were animals of all kinds including a wolf. Shelley went to plead that Byron would allow the child, Allegra, to return to her mother and that he would provide some support for the two of them. Lest any paraphrase of Byron's reaction to this appeal might do him an injustice, we will quote his own words to his half-sister, Augusta Leigh. 'Allegra is well,' he wrote, 'but her mother (whom the Devil confound) came prancing the other day over the Appennines – to see her *shild*; which threw my Venetian loves (who are none of the quietest) into great combustion; and I was in a pucker till I got her to the Euganean hills, where she and the child now are, for the present. I declined seeing her for fear that the consequence might be an addition to the family.' A few weeks later Shelley returned to Venice from the Euganean hills, so obligingly put at his and Clare's disposal by Byron; he was with his wife, Mary, this time and they sought the help of a doctor for their ailing baby. Before they could find the doctor, the baby was dead; she is buried on the Lido.

On the right of the Mocenigo palaces is the Palazzo Contarini delle Figure and on their left the Palazzo Corner-Gheltof, neither of much interest, nor is there much to spend time on until the next *vaporetto* stop up the Grand Canal, S. Angelo. This is by the Palazzo Corner-Spinelli, a very early Renaissance building which is highly regarded – and even tolerated by Ruskin as 'graceful and interesting'.

Now let us return to the *vaporetto* and book to the Ca' d'Oro. We are on a pleasure trip and we need hardly bother with the names of the palaces we pass. The names of most will have fled our memory but those we like will have remained in it.

The Ca' d'Oro is the first stop past the Rialto Bridge and, once under the bridge, the buildings on the left are familiar to us. Those on the right are new to us but we shall be able to study them later today.

We disembark at the Ca' d'Oro, still, probably, in spite of all attempts to ruin it by restoration, the most felicitous Gothic building in Venice. Ruskin thought it was 'quaint' but nevertheless noble, and its destruction, which went on before his eyes, moved him to bitter words. It was the ballet dancer Marie Taglioni who was responsible for this vandalism. She had been given the Ca' d'Oro by a Russian Prince, Alexander Troubetzkoi, who had fallen in love with her when he was thirty-three and she forty-five. While Ruskin was noting that the palace's glorious interior staircase, by far the most interesting Gothic monument of the kind in Venice, was being carried away, piece by piece, and sold for waste marble, his wife Effie was writing home that Troubetzkoi now never left Taglioni's side. His romance with her culminated in his marrying her daughter. It must have been Taglioni who was responsible for the feeling of *déjà vu* which a visit to the Isabella Stewart Gardner house in Boston gives. The columns appear to have been copied so faithfully from the Ca' d'Oro that they might be the originals. That, in fact, is precisely what they are.

It was originally built in 1424-30 (about the same time as the Pitti Palace in Florence: the Renaissance came late to Venice). It was called the Ca' d'Oro because of its abundant gilding and the façade must have looked glorious indeed in its golden coat, richly decorated in all colours; even today the courtyard causes us to catch our breath momentarily at its beauty. The well-head in the courtyard was sold by Taglioni, but at the beginning of this century the palace was bought by a Baron Giorgio Franchetti, who found the well-head and much other stone which

he restored to their original positions. He had inherited from his father that monster by the Accademia Bridge (formerly called the Palazzo Cavalli but now Franchetti after the man who 'restored' it), but refused to live there and devoted himself to the Ca' d'Oro, finally giving it to Venice with all his furniture, tapestries and paintings. Ruskin, no doubt, would have considered he over-restored it but he certainly left it better than did poor Taglioni (who died, bankrupt, in Paddington).

In due course more restoration became necessary and the palace was closed for more than ten years. At last, in 1984, it reopened – though for how long who can say – now with air-conditioning and other modern museum technology and it is mostly devoted to the decorative arts. Do not expect, though, to see how a fifteenth-century Venetian (or even a nineteenth-century dancer) lived; the Ca' d'Oro makes no attempt to do for the Gothic period what the Ca' Rezzonico does for the Renaissance.

Among the many non-Venetian paintings is Mantegna's wonderful and terrible *St. Sebastian*.

This may well spoil our day if we run into it since, terrible as all *St. Sebastians* are, this must surely be unsurpassed in flesh-creeping quality. A couple of Guardis have charm and topographical interest and, if you have come to Venice to look at Flemish pictures and tapestries, this is the place for you. You will even be able to see the remains of one of Giorgione's frescos from the Fondaco dei Tedeschi (*La Nuda*; see p. 107 for the whereabouts of the other surviving fragment) although you will not know a great deal more about Giorgione after seeing it. The views from the windows are of course stupendous. Now let us set out on our walk.

II. Northern Venice. We leave the Ca' d'Oro and are quickly in the Strada Nova which is already familiar to us. A little to our right, on the opposite side of it, is S. Sofia which we remember as the church which has lost its façade and is the point where we entered the Strada Nova. We are not now going to the right, though, which leads to the Rialto Bridge, but to the left and we soon pass the church of S. Felice. Now we cross the Ponte Nicolò Pasqualigo, from which to the left we get a view across the Grand Canal of the Ca' Pesaro, which we have seen from farther down the canal. To the right there is a fine palace, the Dona Giovanelli, and on the left a tablet in the wall commemorating the opening up of the Via Vittorio Emanuele. The top of the map overleaf will show what was involved to connect the street marked 'Rio Terrà' (top left) with the Campo SS. Apostoli on the right. It is hard to realise that even in Ruskin's time this street did not exist.

Soon after crossing the bridge, we will see a delicious old chemist's shop on our left and, if we pop in with a smile just to have a look, we shall be made to feel very welcome. This *farmacia* happens to be the oldest in Venice but there are others as attractive and they are nearly always worth looking at. The *farmacia* has always been used as a meeting place and club by Venetians. You went there to read the papers or see your friends just as often as to buy your *triaca*, which Francis Bacon knew as Venetian treacle. H. V. Morton (in *A Traveller in Italy*) tells us he bought

Canal Grande

Le Fabriche

Pescharia

R. i terra

La Madelena

S. Fosca

No.

S. Felice

Cale delle

Forego da Turcha

Rio di C. Tron

Rio del Mazo

Rio di colato

S. Giacomo dell'Orio

Ruga delli

Rio delli Per

Rio delle

Cale della

Rio delle Torre

S. Gia. san

Cale delli

Rio di

Becca rie

S. Cassan

some quite recently in a chemist's shop called the *Testa d'Oro* near the Rialto Bridge, and even swallowed it. It was a famous cure-all in Nero's time and both the Crusaders and the pilgrims invariably took their 'treacle box' on board ship with them. It used to have sixty ingredients, all publicly displayed before the authorised days when it was compounded under doctors' and health authorities' supervision. John Evelyn saw one of these brewings in 1645. *Triaca* has a venerable and fascinating history.

We turn right at the Campo Santa Fosca and cross another bridge with two pairs of white footprints, such as we saw on the Ponte dei Pugni near S. Barnaba. Evidently this bridge was used for fist fights, we say smugly to ourselves, and indeed it was: it is now the Ponte S. Fosca but it used to be Ponte della Guerra. Over the bridge, we turn left and look ahead where we shall see the entrance of the old Convent of the Servi. The door is almost all that is left but it was once a fine, very early Gothic building. Ruskin complained to his father in 1852 that it was offered to him for sale, as it was or stone by stone, just as he preferred, but he bought nothing. If he had done so, he would have had something more valuable to give the British Museum than his plaster casts of the capitals of the Doge's Palace which must have proved something of an embarrassment (but no longer: they have 'disappeared').

We now turn right along the little Fondamenta de Grimani, right again over another little bridge, then left in front of S. Marziale which, if open, demands a moment to glance at the strange scene in marble under the altar, Venetian baroque at its most charming and idiotic. So on back around the church to the Fondamenta de la Misericordia where we turn right and, at the end of the *fondamenta*, reach a dull building used for storing archives and as the home of an athletic society. It was intended to be the new *scuola* for the brothers of the Misericordia who called in Sansovino for the work – although they already had a fine Gothic *scuola* which we shall see in a moment. We turn left here, just as we reach the bridge, and soon, facing us over the wooden Ponte de l'Abazia, are

the old scuola and the church of the Misericordia.

There is a strange fascination about this lonely
part of Venice where the tourists hardly ever
penetrate, and we may well pause a while to
explore. Otherwise, we turn left and go under a
sottoportico along the Fondamenta dell' Abazia.
We are led over the wooden Ponte dei Muti in
order to pass behind a *squero* but get back to
the *fondamenta* and, just before the next bridge,
we see, on the right, a house with a tablet showing that Tintoretto lived there. Next to it is the
first of four figures we shall see, three of them
Moors who are supposed to have been a Levan-
tine family of three brothers called Mastelli and
who built the Mastelli Palace, starting from
Tintoretto's house and occupying a whole block
with frontages on two canals. The second figure,
with the metal nose, is on the corner and he is
Sior Antonia Rioba, a figure of fame in the city.
There used to be a box beside him into which
you could put accusations against your enemy of
the moment with a fair chance that it would

lead to his imprisonment, or perhaps, if you
were lucky, even to his execution.

We now turn right and are in the Campo dei
Mori from which we see another façade of the
Palazzo Mastelli and the remaining two Moors.
Through a closed gate on the right of the campo
(No. 3381) we see a courtyard, part of which at
any rate must once have been enclosed for it
has a fireplace as well as a well-head and some
strange scraps of sculpture. It is all rather mysterious and the word *Moro*, after which the *campo*
is named, does not elucidate it. As well as meaning Moor, it means mulberry, hence Morea
which is supposed to be mulberry shaped –
Morea, by the way, is the southern island of
Greece, better known as Peloponnese; we hear
much of it in Venice but may not know where it
is. And were the Mastelli brothers Moors or
Moreans? No one knows.

We continue across the campo and cross the
next canal, the Rio della Madonna dell'Orto
and, if we turn right for a moment, we shall be
able to see the north façade of the Mastelli Palace
with its sculpture of a man leading a camel;

because of it, the palace has also been known as the Palazzo Camello; Ruskin knew it by that name and made this beautiful drawing of it.

Returning, we find ourselves outside the Madonna dell' Orto (of the Garden) with its late Gothic façade and lovely cloister. The English have made this church their own, lavishing care and money on its restoration, so in we go to see its four Tintorettos. But we should heed Ruskin's warning: we 'need not hope to derive any pleasure from them without resolute study and then not unless we are accustomed to decipher the thoughts in a picture patiently'. They do not sound at all for us. He could not even persuade his wife to like them. 'John took me to see two large Tintorettos,' she wrote to Rawdon Brown, 'but going in hot to a place like a well to see a death's head crowned with leaves gave me such a shiver that I ran out of the church and I do not intend to return again.' He could not have shown her Cima da Conegliano's *St. John the Baptist*, for the background, anyway, of that could not have failed to enchant her. For once, the saints do not block it all out and, moreover, you can actually see the picture. It is on the right as you enter.

On leaving (not, like Effie, running out of) the church, we turn for a final look at its superb façade. It was originally dedicated to St. Christopher, who stands above the porch, ready to help travellers endure their bad inns, and it was rebuilt in the 1400's, so Ruskin would have called it Renaissance Gothic, like the Porta della Carta or the Ca' d'Oro. It really was worth the journey.

We now turn right, pass a first wooden bridge and before reaching a second one, glance into the Corte del Cavallo on the right. This is where Verrochio had his studio and workshop and where Leopardi, after Verrochio's death, cast his statue of Colleoni and his horse, which we saw outside SS. Giovanni e Paolo.

The second wooden bridge leads to the Calle Loredan and it is our intention to re-cross the three *rii* we have already crossed, each with its *fondamenta*. The first is the Fondamenta della Sensa and, if it is not between twelve and four, I must ask you to make a digression. Turn right along this *fondamenta*, cross a bridge from which you get a vista of the lagoon, and turn right again at the second calle (del Capitelo). You will now re-cross the Rio della Madonna del Orto and be outside the church of S. Alvise. It has an intriguing *trompe-l'œil* painted ceiling, a Tiepolo Calvary, said to be one of his best, and two other Tiepolos, surely among his worst. But it also has the 'Baby Carpaccios' over which poor Ruskin made such as fool of himself for once. He was convinced these little pictures were by Carpaccio, although Carpaccio would have been only eight when they were painted, and said he would have given anything to know their real history.

I cannot resist reproducing (opposite) *The Meeting of Solomon and the Queen of Sheba* for Ruskin was bewitched by the 'exquisite strangeness' of the little wooden bridge over a ditch; 'the question seems to be which shall first set foot on it,' he wrote. Years later, in almost the last letter he ever wrote, he was thanking an old lady who was a neighbour for telling him the true meaning. It was, she explained, from this bridge that the True Cross was to be made and the Queen of Sheba had a vision of the future that awaited

SALAMON

its timbers just as she was about to cross it. She is telling King Solomon what she has seen and why she will not cross.

The eight little pictures were in fact painted by Lazzaro Bastiani, or one of his followers, to decorate an organ. It is true that Carpaccio was a pupil of Bastiani's – but not at eight!

Let us, if we have been to S. Alvise, now return down the Calle del Capitelo, cross the bridge by a surprising and rather desirable modern house into the Calle de la Malvasia and so reach the Fondamenta Ormesini where we turn left. If we chose to miss S. Alvise when we left the Madonna del Orto, we go straight on from Calle Loredan (where a hotel, Ai Mori D'Oriente, offers us a seat by the canal) down Calle del Forno and reach the Fondamenta Ormesini, wehre we turn right. If it is time for refreshment in earnest, the Osteria Bacco here provides memorable fish.

Whichever way we reached the wooden bridge between the Calle del al Malvasia and the Calle del Forno, we now cross it and find ourselves in Rio Terrà Farsetti. If we are anxious to see the two Ghettos of Venice, the old Ghetto and the new, we turn off this *calle* to the right. There is nothing to be seen, though, except a Jewish Community Museum and the highest houses in the city. The word Ghetto is another of Venice's gifts to the world, like Lido, Arsenal and sequin. The Getto, from *gettare*, to cast, was, until the beginning of the sixteenth century, the place where the shot was cast, and it was here. Jews had been in Venice by this time for two hundred years, but mostly on the Giudecca to which they had *almost* certainly given the name. The Venetians liked having the Jews among them (they had much in common with them and, apart from finding them *simpatico*, found they could make money out of them, the quickest way to a Venetian's heart), and in 1517 they moved the Getto to a more convenient situation and handed the area over to the Jews. In time it became the Ghetto and the name spread to other Jewish quarters throughout the world. It must seem as odd to the Venetians that there should be ghettoes in Poland as that there should be a Lido in Hyde Park, but it is thus that words develop.

We continue along the Rio Terrà Farsetti, or return to it if we found the expedition to the Ghetto irresistible, and almost imperceptibly the Strada Nova joins us. Now it is the Rio Terrà S. Leonardo that we are in and we are by no means alone in it.

We continue as far as the great Canareggio bridge which we cross and gratefully find the Hotel Marte at the corner with its few chairs and tables outside for us to indulge in our aperitif. Now for our favourite kind of sightseeing.

III. The Canareggio. The Canareggio (or Cannaregio or Cannareggio: authority can be found for all forms of spelling) is the most important canal of Venice after the Grand Canal, but far less important than it used to be before the railway bridge was built. It was by this route that the traveller from Mestre entered Venice (the Mestre *traghetto* stop was on the *fondamenta* opposite us) : the traveller from Fusina came in via the Giudecca. The name came from *canne*, or reeds, which are said to have grown here in prodigious quantity and it applies not only to the canal but

to a whole *sestiere* which must have been marshland at one time but was gradually reclaimed and divided into the regular strips of land with canals between them which stand out so distinctly on our map. We can look down it and see its two *fondamente*, flanked by palaces, but we need not walk along them. We shall see them from our *motoscafo* when we do our expedition on the Number 52 and today we need look only towards the Grand Canal.

From our seat we can see the Canareggio frontage of the Palazzo Labia and, beyond it, the *campo* and church of S. Geremia (another of these Jewish saints). As for the bridge itself, there was certainly one here, built of wood, in 1285, and a stone one in 1580. The present one was built in 1777 and is called the Ponte delle Guglie, after its four obelisks, as well as the Ponte di Canareggio.

To see the land entrance of the Palazzo Labia we must go round to the Campo S. Geremia where it occupies the whole of one side, another side being taken up by the church. The Labia Palace started as the show-place of a millionaire and ended its life – as a private house anyway –

in the same way. It is hard to say who gained most marks for showing off in it, its first or last private owner. The first is said to have celebrated one occasion with a feast, after which he threw golden dishes into the canal, shouting, with characteristic millionaire's wit, 'Le abia, o non le abia, saró sempre Labia' which means 'Whether I have them or not, I shall still be Labia'. Next day they were brought up from the canal by means of the net which had been laid for their rescue. The last, a Mexican millionaire, completed in the 1950's the restorations begun by the last Labias shortly before, and which it certainly needed: it had been described as silent and desolate in 1909 and was damaged when an ammunition ship blew up in the Second World War. He proved a worthy successor to the Labias and on his death the palace was taken by a broadcasting corporation. They have looked after it beautifully and, if you choose the right moment, will let you in to see the palace and some at least of its immensely gay frescos by Tiepolo.

We must stroll down past the palace's water entrance to the end of the Fondamenta de Ca

Labia and look out on to the Grand Canal, where Canaletto wanted us to think his picture, reproduced opposite, was painted from. In fact, the drawings for it were done from the conveniently placed Riva di Biasio on the other side of the Canal and they were drawn, as is nearly always the case with Canaletto, from several different viewpoints, the painting itself being built up in the studio. The statue and balcony in the picture have provided a nice problem for art historians. They are not in Visentini's first engraving of Canaletto's painting, nor could they be since the engraving was published in 1735 and the statue and balcony were not erected until 1742. How, then, do they come to be in the painting? The answer, no doubt, is that the owner, Joseph Smith, made Canaletto add them at a later date, nor was this the only occasion for such meticulousness on Smith's part (see p. 195).

There is nothing of interest on the opposite side of the Grand Canal, and only the huge Vendramin Calergi Palace down on the left on our side, so we go back to the bridge and continue our walk, turning left into the Campo

S. Geremia. From there we find the name of our street has changed again, this time to Rio Terrà Lista di Spagna. An eighteenth-century map shows it bearing the same name, but then it was a canal; the word *lista* indicated that it was in the neighbourhood of an embassy; in this case the Spanish Embassy which was nearby. The Barbari detail above shows the Canareggio and S. Geremia with part of the Grand Canal.

It is probably lunch-time by now and we are in a district abounding in small restaurants, none of them, unfortunately, enabling us to sit and contemplate the Grand Canal which is so tantalizingly close. Do not despair. We continue along the Lista di Spagna, passing a Gothic doorway with a carving above it bearing a crest supported

by two cherubs; this was the Palazzo Morosini, famous for its gardens and its courtyard. We soon reach the modern Hotel Principe and, a little further on, the restaurant Povoledo. Both have tables by the Canal and provide us with a splendid view of the Grand Canal. We can see down it as far as the Palazzo Vendramin Calergi, and up as far as the railway station and stone bridge.

We may remember (p. 77) that this, like the Accademia Bridge, was built in the 1930's to replace a hideous iron one, and that both are of the same proportions and both by the same architect.

If, after lunch, we want to rest our feet we could go to the station stop and get to S. Marco by Nos. 1 (14 stops, 40 minutes), 2 (6 stops, 31 minutes), 41 (6 stops, 26 minutes), or 51 (4 stops,

23 minutes). If lunch has refreshed us we will continue to walk, at any rate to the Rialto Bridge.

We return the way we came – all the way to the point where we entered into Rio Terrà S. Leonardo from the Rio Terrà Farsetti. We may well wonder how the citizens of Venice managed before this became a *rio terrà* for it must always have been a busy street for pedestrians. The explanation may be found from the section of the Barbari view and that of the eighteenth-century map on p. 187 from which it is evident that, although a canal took the place of the street, there was always a fairly wide *fondamenta* beside it. The point at which the two impor-tant *rii*, now *rii terrà*, S. Leonardo and Farsetti meet is called the Campo Anconetta, although there is no street sign to indicate it. Here we turn off to the right down the Rio Terrà del Cristo, and then into the Campo S. Marcuola with its church and *vaporetto* stop.

S. Marcuola is another of the city churches where the money (or interest) ran out before the façade could be finished and it never has been finished. How SS. Ermagora e Fortunato,

the church's true name, became S. Marcuola I cannot tell you, but we have not come here to see the church. We have come to look across the Grand Canal at what appears to be, perhaps, a fire station of grey stone built in the 1920's.

IV. The Fondaco dei Turchi. It is, in fact, nothing of the sort. It is the Fondaco dei Turchi, formerly the Casa del Duca di Ferrara, and, improbable as it may seem, those stones are among the oldest in Venice. It was built soon after 1200 (and perhaps even before) as a private house and, from 1381 onwards, was in great demand by the Republic as quarters for distin-guished visitors and their suites. By 1621, it must have started to decay fairly badly for it was then bought by the Republic and let to the Turkish merchants as a warehouse when it acquired the name of Fondaco dei Turchi. Its great days were over and you can see opposite what it looked like by 1720. Worse was to come, though, for by Ruskin's day it had become 'a ghastly ruin' and the photograph on p. 190 shows it much as he saw it. It was then a tobacco store, although it

is hard to see how anything as perishable as tobacco could have been stored in it, and in 1860 the 'restorations' began.

This, then, is one of those palaces which made 'a city of graceful arcades and gleaming walls, veined with azure and warm with gold and fretted with marble', in Ruskin's words, for we are assured that it now looks much as it did originally and much of the material of which it is built is said to be original.

Ruskin spent weeks measuring and studying every detail of the building, the bases of its columns and, above all, their capitals, its sculptures, its elevation, its parapets – everything. Overleaf is an exquisite drawing by him of part of the building, the top right-hand part, which has not come out in the photograph as well as the rest. How would you have it? As it is now or as it was then, the 'covering stones torn away from it like the shroud from a corpse; its walls rent into a thousand chasms . . . the seams and hollows choked with clay and whitewash, oozing and trickling over the marble – itself blanched into dusty decay by the frosts of centuries . . .'

and so on, sentence after mighty sentence of noble invective against those who were leaving it to 'fester to its fall'? How could they be blamed if they finally did what was demanded of them and 'restored' it?

On the left of the Fondaco dei Turchi are the Depositi del Megio, the old granaries used for storing millet, and then comes the Palazzo Belloni-Battagia, seventeenth-century, the Palazzo Tron, sixteenth, and two Gothic palaces, one on either side of a garden which was the site of one of the many Contarini palaces.

On our own side of the Grand Canal, from the pontoon, we see on our left the huge Vendramin Calergi Palace (Plate 27). This was one of the first Renaissance palaces built in Venice, begun more than half a century after the new fashion had become virtually a commonplace in Florence. It served as the home of the Duchesse de Berry in the Ruskins' time, and after that of Richard Wagner, who died there. It is now the Winter Casino. Next below it, but out of sight, is the Palazzo Marcello where a less illustrious and more pathetic creature, Frederic Rolfe,

Baron Corvo, died in 1913.

Now we turn away, after a glance up the Grand Canal where we see S. Geremia, with its mysteriously dated statue in front of it, and beyond, where the Scalzi church has come into sight. The dull, stone palace between the two is called Palazzo Flangini and was never finished. We turn right over the bridge crossing the Rio di S. Marcuola. This leads us behind the Palazzo Vendramin Calergi and back to our old Strada Nova, here the Rio Terrà de la Maddalena, where we turn right. Just before we cross the next bridge, we turn and look at the Campo della Maddalena with its much photographed ancient houses with their Venetian chimneys, and its fine Renaissance well-head.

We then continue along the Strada Nova as far as S. Felice, which we know well, and opposite the church we find a Calle del Traghetto. This used to lead to two *traghetti*, one going straight across the Grand Canal to the Palazzo Corner della Regina, the public pawnshop, and the Ca' Pesaro, the museum of modern art; the other crossing at a slant to the Pescheria, or fish market. *Traghetti* come and go these days and both had gone the last time I sought their services. In order to reach the Pescheria we may have to go back to the Strada Nova and continue along it to the Campo S. Sofia where an almost certain *traghetto* will be awaiting us.

After the delights of a *traghetto* crossing, we shall probably by now be ready for the Rialto Bridge and home, but for those who wish to explore the only interesting parts of Venice not already covered by our walks this would be a good starting point. They would turn right and away from the Grand Canal along the Calle del Campanile at the end of the fondamenta and find themselves at S. Cassiano. From there, they would find their way by map to the Campo S. Maria Mater Domini, equal in the variety and picturesqueness of its buildings to the Campo della Maddalena which we have just left. Judicious use of the map and a few smiling enquiries (answered by the inevitable '*sempre dritto*') will then lead to S. Giacomo dell' Orio, a church which was already being *re*built in 1225. From here they could strike south-east and, via the

Campo S. Agostino and Campo S. Polo, reach the Campo S. Aponal and the Rialto Bridge or continue west and ultimately reach the vast red seventeenth- and eighteenth-century building of S. Nicolò da Tolentino. This stands close to the Papadopoli gardens and the Piazzale Roma from which home can easily be reached by *vaporetto*. Experienced walkers in Venice, as we have now become, will need no guide book to explore this neighbourhood. Each will find his own favourite and personal canal or palace – probably only to find later that it has been commemorated in numerous old photographs and water colours.

V. From the Pescheria. We who are making for the Rialto Bridge from the *traghetto* stop now have a splendid view of the Ca' d'Oro and of the palaces between it and the bridge. There are two other Gothic palaces, the Pesaro and the Sagredo, then the Campo S. Sofia with its *traghetto*, of which we may just have made use. Then comes a Foscari palace with fine windows and, next but one, the Michiel dalle Colonne (after its colonnade) and the Michiel del Brusa (after its fire, which took place in 1774), both late seventeenth- and eighteenth-century.

The next palace is the Mangilli-Valmarana (on the left of the Rio degli SS. Apostoli, a canal which would take us straight out to the Fondamente Nuove). This was the home, from 1740 onwards, of Consul Joseph Smith, Canaletto's greatest patron, who finally sold his collection of fifty paintings and a hundred and forty drawings by Canaletto to George III, in whose Royal Collection they still remain. In 1743 Smith decided to rebuild his palace and employed for the purpose Antonio Visentini, who was not only an architect but also a painter and engraver whose engravings of one of Canaletto's Grand Canal series, now in the Royal Collection, had been published in 1735. Nine years older than Canaletto, Visentini died fourteen years after him at the age of ninety-four. The work on Consul Smith's palace was not finished until 1751 and a few years later Canaletto returned to Venice after his ten years in England. His painting of the Grand Canal from the Rialto Bridge which showed the Palazzo Mangilli-Valmarana was in Smith's collection and of course included the old-fashioned façade – it was, indeed, one of those engraved by Visentini in 1735. It would never do for a gentleman to own a picture depicting his house with an out-of-date façade so Canaletto was called in to repaint this tiny part of his picture. He performed his minute commission with such care and skill that it was not until two hundred years later that Sir Michael Levey of the National Gallery detected it.

On the other side of the Rio dei SS. Apostoli is the Ca' da Mosto. This was built originally in the thirteenth century, and by the time the pilgrims were arriving in Venice, in the fifteenth, it was an inn, the famous Leon Bianco or White Lion. We saw it behind the Rialto Bridge in Carpaccio's *Miracle of the Holy Cross*. It ceased being an inn by the beginning of the nineteenth century, and when we read of any visitor staying at the Leon Bianco after that, it was not here but at a hotel below the Rialto Bridge, just beyond where the Riva del Carbon ends. It was in this later Leon Bianco, for instance, that Turner stayed on his first visit to Venice.

We continue walking towards the Rialto Bridge making our way across the Campo de la Pescheria, but keeping as close to the Canal as possible. The next canal we see across the Grand Canal is the Rio S. Giovanni Crisostomo which would take us direct to the Arsenal or, if we turned off it down the Rio S. Lorenzo, to the Riva degli Schiavoni. After that, we see the Campiello del Remer, with its remains of Byzantine arches where we stood and looked up at the Rialto Bridge, then nothing of great interest until we see another *rio* and part of the Fondaco dei Tedeschi. The *rio* is one we have already crossed two or three times and, as our map shows, it ends by passing underneath the Bridge of Sighs. The Fondaco dei Tedeschi is now the Post Office but, just as the Fondaco dei Turchi was given to the Turks for their warehouse, so this site was given to the Germans before the end of the thirteenth century. (*Tedeschi* are Germans, and it was Tedeschi that Veronese got into trouble over for putting them into his *Feast in the House of Levi*).

Where there are Germans, there are sausages and beer, and so it was in 1450 for there was by then a large restaurant just by the Fondaco dei Tedeschi which specialised in these. German pilgrims stayed, not at the Leon Bianco, but at the Flute which was close by (we may remember Brother Fabri's description of its dog on page 107). In 1505 the Fondaco dei Tedeschi was burnt out and the new one was painted on the outside. By whom? By Titian on the Rialto front and by Giorgione on the canal front. Nothing but the best for those Germans. A few pink shadows could still be seen in Canaletto's time, and can be made out in Plate 17.

We return and pass to the right of those dull New and Old Buildings of the Rialto, the Fabbriche Nuove (1550) and the Fabbriche Vecchie (the same period but *vecchie*, old, because they replaced others). We also pass the Palace of the Camerlenghi, the City Treasurers. All are still civic buildings of one kind or another. We shall also have passed through the fish and vegetable markets and find ourselves in the Ruga dei Oresi, the Street of the Goldsmiths. We have seen something more than the Rialto Bridge. We have seen the Rialto, Venice's kitchen, office and back parlour, just as the Piazza is its front parlour or, as Napoleon said, its drawing-room.

Having made our way through the markets we turn left into the Campo di Rialto with the church of S. Giacomo di Rialto, built in the twelfth century for the merchants of Rialto, and the Bridge in front of us, rather surprisingly, and almost unrecognizably. On our left is the Colonna del Bando, used, like the Pietra del Bando in the Piazza, for announcements but in this case supported by the Gobbo (hunchback) di Rialto. The *sottoportico* behind the column is 'del Banco Giro', a fairly recent name to most of us in England, but the bank of that name was founded in Venice in 1157. We cross the Rialto Bridge, wondering, as always, which side provides the more delectable view.

I have walked you far enough. Wherever you are staying, you can be home in ten minutes from here, either on foot, if near the Riva, or by water if near the Grand Canal. In any case, there is no more sight-seeing for today.

*Around Venice
and the Islands of the Lagoon*

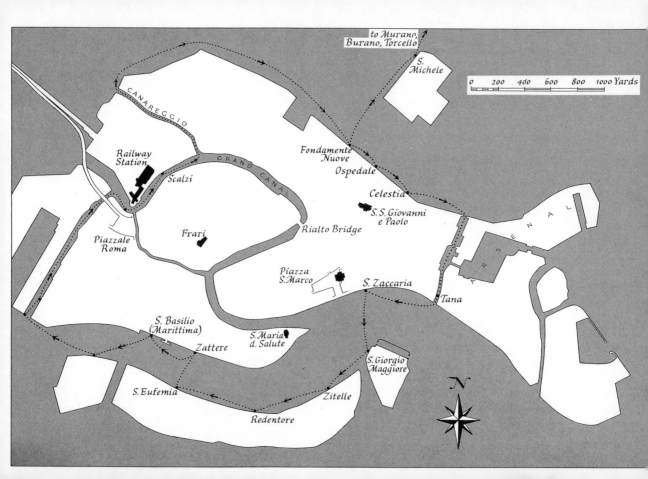

Around Venice
and the Islands of the Lagoon

I. The Ancient Settlements. By now, we may well feel we know something of Venice – and we do: we have seen more of it than most Venetians. But it is Rialto that we have seen, one only of the twelve lagoon townships which combined to form the State of Venice in four hundred and something (midday on 25 March 421 James Morris tells us the old chronicles date it, a Friday according to his perpetual calendar: we must be satisfied with something less precise). Let us consider the other eleven.

Grado is not in our lagoon at all, but the next one up towards Trieste. It is a flourishing seaside resort now and near Aquileia, an important city on the mainland at the time of the barbarian invasions. We must go to Aquileia next time we are in this neighbourhood.

Bibbione, Caorle, Heraclea and Jesolo are all on the mainland to the north-east of us – that part of the mainland which throws down a peninsula, almost, but not quite, joining on to the Lido. Between them, the sea enters the lagoon forming the great Porto di Lido, the main gateway to Venice. There is a fine church at Caorle, nothing to be seen at Bibbione or Heraclea, and Jesolo is almost worth a visit as an act of penance. Within a few years it has grown from an insignificant village to a town of glass and concrete hotels, smart shops stuffed with merchandise someone has described as *tripe à la mode* and all the necessary appurtenances of modern mass sunbathing. Half the arrivals at Venice airport in the summer are bound for Jesolo. The whole thing exists for a few weeks only; then it becomes a ghost city like Klondike – until the following year when it all starts again. Jesolo's original refugees from the mainland stayed longer than today's.

Poveglia is the island behind S. Servolo, once a home for the aged and poor, now one of sixteen islands abandoned since 1968. Malamocco is now a village on the lagoon side of the Lido which we pass on the way to Chioggia. It was much dreaded for centuries by voyagers from areas suspected of the plague for they were often compelled to wait on board there for a month in quarantine. Originally, though, Malamocco was an island nearby, no one knows quite where. It was the first capital of the new State before it moved to Rialto.

Chioggia and Sottomarina are at the tip of the peninsula coming up north from the mainland, just as the peninsula with Jesolo on it (and Punta Sabbioni at its tip) comes down south. The islands of Lido and Pellestrina close the gap between Chioggia and Punta Sabbioni. (I know I have referred to this before, more than once. Many visitors, though, leave Venice without any sense of its position as an island, or series of islands, in the centre of a lagoon, and some consciousness of its geographical situations is essential to a true sympathy, or sense of unity, with the city. Forgive the repetition.) Chioggia is well worth a visit one day by the tourist boat referred to in Appendix A, and there is a bridge from Chioggia across to Sottomarina, now trying to rival Jesolo as a resort. An after-lunch stroll to the Duomo of Chioggia, before the boat returns (or before one sets off on that extraordinary boat-bus-ferry-bus-boat expedition) will enable us to see all of Chioggia we need, and to enjoy its undoubted charm.

This leaves only Murano and Torcello of the ancient townships (Burano was not one of them) and these we must visit. We should, moreover, land on the two islands we have looked across to so often, S. Giorgio Maggiore and the Giudecca. We have seen nothing of the west side of the city, the true Port of Venice. And we spared ourselves the walk along the Canareggio Canal knowing we should return to it. Clearly, the moment has come for us to begin our tour around the island.

II. Around Venice. In previous editions of this book I eulogised the No. 5, always known as the *Circolare* to Venetians. Today's readers are less fortunate: the No. 5 is now nothing more than a seasonal Murano service, and we must use both the No. 2 and the No. 41/42 or the No. 51/52 if we are to circle the island and be able to disembark where we wish. Our map continues to show the route of the No. 5 service in the hope that the ACTV will see sense and introduce it again some day. The No. 2 is mainly a tourist service, while the Nos. 41/42 and the Nos. 51/52 are a *motoscafo* service and follows some of the route taken by the old No. 5. The former go to Murano, the latter to Lido; Nos. 41 and 51 go anti-clockwise, and Nos. 42 and 52 clockwise. Naturally there are extra subtleties that only prolonged study will reveal.

These boats sail every twenty minutes or so during the day, if we may apply the word sail to anything so modern and efficient as a *vaporetto* or *motoscafo*. The cost of the round trip, including a visit to Murano, is little enough, although it will cost a great deal more if we leave the boat and proceed by the next one at a number of stations, as we fully intend to do. We would be well advised, therefore, to take a daily or weekly ticket, or invest in a Venice Card (which also gives reductions on some museum entrance fees) so that we may disembark freely without worrying about the expense.

We must now board the No. 2 at the S. Zaccaria stop on the Riva degli Schiavoni, opposite the Danieli Hotel. Its first stop after S. Zaccaria is S. Giorgio Maggiore, where we disembark.

S. Giorgio Maggiore is today an Island of Culture, thanks to the generosity of Count Cini to whose Cini Foundation it has been leased and who has done much to restore the island to something of its original beauty and splendour. Culture now oozes from every brick and lurks behind every tree, and with the Arts go the

Crafts. Music, architecture, drama, and the history of art are all studied side by side with typography, seamanship, tailoring and carpentry. There is an open-air theatre in a garden of strange beauty, a fine refectory by Palladio, with a Veronese which Napoleon thought it worthwhile to steal, and a library of considerable fame by Longhena. The whole undertaking gives an impression of intense culture, intense civilization and intense cold. Let us, instead, enter the church, in spite of Ruskin's contempt for it.

It is also pretty cold but we shall find the carvings on the choir stalls highly exhilarating. They depict, in wood, scenes from the story of St. Benedict whose life seems to have been eventful and interesting. Unless we wish to study the Tintorettos in the chancel, we should next ascend the campanile in the charge of a monk who will be justifiably proud of the splendid modern lift; everything on S. Giorgio Maggiore is of the best.

Experienced topographers of Venice as we now are will need no guide to the scene from the top of the campanile. Here we see Venice almost as Barbari saw it – not quite, of course, as he was drawing from an imaginary aeroplane looking down on the scene which included the island and campanile of S. Giorgio Maggiore itself. Nor was it even the same campanile, although it looks much like it in the woodcut. The present church was not started until 1566 and the belfry and steeple of the campanile came two hundred years later, although the base is older. Otherwise the island seems to have looked very much as it does now. There is a detail from the Barbari view opposite (which is, in fact, a continuation towards the right of the detail shown on p. 28) and which shows the near prospect. S. Zaccaria with its cloister is in the centre and, to its left, the Danieli Hotel.

We can judge how long we have to spend on the campanile by noting when the No. 2 leaves S. Zaccaria for the island, and in due course we board it again. Its first stop is now the Zitelle on the island of Giudecca, a dull church. If we want an apéritif at the Hotel Cipriani, we could land here, but we would do better to take the hotel's own (free) boat another day from near

Harry's Bar. We could then see how a civilized country-house atmosphere can be combined with the utmost luxury. It has an immense heated saltwater swimming pool and as many staff as guests when the hotel is full – more when it is less than full. If necessary, it is worth living on sandwiches (always good in Venice anyway) for a few days to indulge in a meal here.

We are now on the island of Giudecca which, since five canals run through it, could be called

six islands. The next stop is at Palladio's Church of the Redeemer (Il Redentore). Palladio lovers will certainly want to examine the Redentore, perhaps his best church; others may find the idea inviting of a stroll in this area, generally free from tourists. After the next stop, Palanca, the captain will now appear to change his mind and go back again. It is only done in order to reach the first stop on the Zattere, by the Rio di S. Trovaso which we remember, and at the stop after that, S. Basilio (Marittima), we shall disembark and stretch our legs. We have already visited the Zattere, although not as far west as we are now. There are three churches here, each justifying a visit more than many of the better known churches nearer the centre of the city.

We can best reach the first, S. Sebastiano, by keeping to our side of the nearest canal and walking up its *fondamenta* before we cross the bridge leading to the church. It is Veronese's church, gaily decorated by him, and his burial place; it was here that he first made his name at the age of twenty-eight and was ranked with Tintoretto or even Titian who was eighty.

Within sight of S. Sebastiano, to the northwest, is the church of Angelo Raffaele which offers us the attractive organ panels by (almost certainly) Gianantonio Guardi; Francesco Guardi worked with this elder brother until his death, only then taking to view-painting although over fifty. From there we may cross the *rio* and walk along its fondamenta to the church of S. Nicolo dei Mendicoli, probably the most worthwhile of all the three churches. Here is a miracle of enlight-

ened restoration, largely carried out by the British Venice in Peril fund who have transformed the ancient parish church into one of the brightest jewels of Venice.

Now we go back to S. Basilio to continue on the No. 2. We return to the Giudecca for a moment and then proceed through some very unpromising territory to emerge at a point which will seem familiar if we entered the city by car. We will be at the Piazzale Roma and if we did not come by car, and we are fortunate enough not to have seen it before, we can commiserate with those who did.

Here it is useless for us to try to recapture the past. At the first bridge we pass under on the *motoscafo*, the one before the road bridge, is the church of S. Andrea. Ruskin used to come here to enjoy the view of the Euganean hills near Padua and the sunset. Well, the sun does still set. Immediately before the road bridge is S. Chiara, or rather the nineteenth-century building which took its place. We can see the island of S. Chiara, as it then was, in the Barbari drawing opposite, just by the P (for *ponente* = west) on the left-hand side. We turn right; here we are at the entrance to the Grand Canal. We stop to pick up the unfortunate car drivers or bus passengers and then pass the entrance to the Rio Nuovo, the short cut to the lower reach of the Grand Canal, on our right. How different it all looks from Francesco Guardi's lovely painting reproduced in Plates 28 and 29, showing the church of S. Lucia and other buildings which were demolished and supplanted by the railway station. Only the church of the Scalzi and some buildings beyond it remain. We are reminded how we

have been spoilt by finding so much of Venice left as it was. Now we are back in Venice and at the railway station we now leave the No. 2 and catch either the No. 42 or the No. 52.

After the station stop we proceed down the Grand Canal with the church of the Scalzi (barefoot friars) on our left and S. Simeone Piccolo, with its green copper roof, on the right (the architect must have had the Pantheon in mind). We go under the stone bridge, past the Principe Hotel after which we turn left at S. Geremia and the Palazzo Labia to enter the Canareggio

Canal. We pass under the Ponte delle Guglie and stop on the Fondamenta di Canareggio opposite the Hotel di Marte where we sat. We are at the spot where, for centuries, the traveller from Mestre had his first sight of Venice. Picture him disembarking at this spot – with no Rio Terrà S. Leonardo to lead him on foot straight to the Rialto Bridge.

Now we can journey down the Canareggio Canal in comfort and if we are on the No. 52 we might well disembark at the next stop for a quarter of an hour.

Naturally, a number of Venetians built their palaces on this important canal. We have already passed two of the biggest which are side by side on the far side of the bridge of three arches: the Palazzo Manfrini and the Palazzo Savorgnan. The Palazzo Savorgnan was once upon a time well known for its garden, but then this was the district for gardens. Between these palaces and the bridge is the Campo S. Giobbe with its church and, formerly, a convent as well. The convent was suppressed in 1812 and its vineyard and gardens turned into the city's Botanical Gardens.

The Palazzo Surian, which is on the side of the canal where we disembarked, just by the bridge, also had a famous garden; Rousseau lived in it while he was secretary to the French Ambassador in Venice.

We now return to await the next No. 52 which now passes the public abattoir at the end of the canal and then turns into the northern lagoon. To the left we see the railway bridge and opposite us the little island of S. Secondo, prominent on Barbari's drawing and the scene of bitter fighting in 1849. The monastery shown by Barbari has long disappeared and the island was abandoned in 1961.

Now we pass round the north tip of Venice and before long the cemetery island of S. Michele comes into view. Both the No. 42 and the No. 52 now stop at S. Alvise, and then at Orto, which we might already know from Walk 4. The campanile with the round dome which we see on the right belongs to the Madonna dell' Orto, so we are very near Verrochio's studio which we saw the site of. Just past it is a low house known as the Casino degli Spiriti, a sixteenth-century palace once the scene of great entertainments, and then comes the Sacca della Misericordia which we saw from the Misericordia abbey (a *sacca* is a stretch of water open on one side only into which more than one canal empties its waters, but it is also used to describe a place where the water encroaches and forms a little bay).

We then see the campanile of the Gesuiti and come to a stop at the Fondamente Nuove opposite the bar we may have patronized on Walk 2. Here we must reach a decision on our route: if we stay on our No. 42 it will take us to Murano before continuing round Venice; we might prefer to change onto one that has already been to Murano. The No. 52 will not go to Murano, but will add a long excursion to Lido to its journey round the city.

Let us assume we decide to go to Murano. We will have time to compare today's scene with the Barbari drawing (p. 148). SS. Giovanni e Paola was, we see, then on the lagoon and so was the Scuola di S. Marco. All the land now between them and the Gesuiti is, therefore, reclaimed from the water and we can understand how Titian's house, now well inland, had its garden sloping down to the lagoon.

The next stop is S. Michele (Cimitero). The elegant white façade of the church was the first Renaissance building to be completed in Venice, having been begun in 1469 – a hundred years before Shakespeare was born.

III. Murano. At the first of Murano's stops, Colonna, we have to make a decision – whether to visit a glass factory or not. If so, we disembark here and turn right and shall have no difficulty whatever in achieving our objective.

The making of glass is certainly a very curious process. It must also be very difficult, although the end product reminds us of Dr. Johnson's comment on a violin piece he had just heard played and which he was told was very difficult: 'I would that it were impossible.' It is quite astonishing that anything so highly regarded throughout the world for so many centuries should be of such uniform hideousness, and we cannot blame the modern designers. A visit to the Murano Glass Museum may well confirm that, with very few exceptions, it has always been the same. Nevertheless it is a curious process, and if we have the time we should see it being performed. If we leave without buying anything, we shall not be set upon, nor shall we be quite the first to do so. It may be wiser to tip the guide generously rather than let him earn the commission on some purchase of ours which we may come to regret when we get home.

We now aim at the fifth stop of our No. 52 on Murano, Museo, either by remaining on board or finding our own way on foot with the aid of a map. If we do get into the new glass museum we must certainly ensure that we keep time and energy for the church of S. Donato, a few steps further on. It is a very remarkable church.

It is almost as old as St. Mark's and its floor is its great glory. We are not going to do the 'hard day's work' in it that Ruskin warned his reader he was in for nor shall we fall into the trap Ruskin did of thinking the undulations of the floor were deliberately contrived to imitate the waves of the sea. They are, in fact, due entirely to uneven subsidences but the effect is glorious and, if this is not enough, we have a spellbinding mosaic over the altar of a Madonna praying against a golden background. Once outside, we walk round the cathedral and examine its apse – and now, unless we want to go on to Burano and Torcello (in which case we must find our way to the next stop, Faro, the lighthouse), we wait for a *motoscafo* to take us back to the Fondamente Nuove for the completion of our circle. If it is lunchtime the best thing we can do is to find a promising looking restaurant (say, the Antica Trattoria) and pray to St. Christopher in the words of Brother Fabri (p. 146). If we want to see the main street of Murano we cross two bridges and find ourselves on a canal with a *fondamenta* on either side. Here once stood all the glass factories now scattered over the island. At the end is the boat stop Colonna.

Until fairly recently the journey eastwards from the Fondamente Nuove held the great excitement of doing nothing less than entering the mysterious Arsenal itself. It was an eerie experience for the longstanding habitué of Venice to be entering the Arsenal for the first time. He has been so used to signs as he approached its precincts proclaiming that it was *vietato* to take one more step that he expected at least a warning shot across the bows of the *motoscafo* as it unconcernedly turned and entered the forbidden territory. The tourist making his first visit to Venice can have felt no apprehension at all; he would have found it hard to believe those long ranges of deserted shipyards could have harboured any secrets of crucial importance for a very long while.

Nor, of course, have they (unless the re-routing of the *motoscafo* is more significant than we might suspect). The last *Bucintoro* was built in the Arsenal in 1724 and this was the one which was destroyed by Napoleon's men seventy-three years later. Nothing much happened meanwhile and when Goethe was allowed into the Arsenal in 1786, he found it 'like visiting some old family which, though past its prime, still shows signs of life'. The only signs of life during the following two centuries would have been some menial repair work for the Austrians and the maintenance of the *vaporetti* (although it boasted of being able to tackle a modern tanker if required). But what a prime it has passed! When Dante wanted his readers to understand what Inferno was like in 1307 he compared it with the Arsenal which was already being expanded to cope with its work. Pero Tafur in 1438 gave up: he just did not know how to describe what he saw there. Casola in 1494 found it an almost incredible thing to one who has not yet seen it.

And now? I have to admit that all that one could see were the mighty walls and – could that have been a tennis court? It was. But we could tell our children that we had been inside the Arsenal – and now it may be that they will never follow us.

Nowadays the No. 42 more prosaically circumnavigates the island, if such a magical journey could ever be anything but poetry. Round Castello and past the Biennale gardens it takes us, and then to the Arsenale boat stop. Just afterwards we pass the Pietà. It was founded, Tafur tells us, with a hundred wet-nurses to suckle the babes of Venetian wives, long separated from their merchant husbands and urged by their fleshly lusts, who otherwise took the simple course of throwing their offspring out of the window into the sea as soon as they were delivered.

And so we are back where we started at S. Zaccaria.

IV. Burano and Torcello. We must now return to the Fondamente Nuove, either on foot or by Nos. 41/42 or 51/52. There we board an LN service which leaves twice an hour, first for the Faro stop at Murano and then for the forty-minute journey to Mazzorbo. There we disembark and walk to Burano, where there is a regular boat to Torcello.

Mazzorbo speaks for itself. It offers a pleasant trattoria (opposite the boat stop), a Grand Canal, a Ca' d'Oro and a church with ivy-covered campanile, none showing any evidence of the island's former grandeur when it was rich in gardens and palaces. We turn left at the boat station and follow the path which leads over a high bridge to Burano (we could go in the other direction and reach the same bridge if we preferred: there is nothing to it). At the Burano boat station we turn right and are soon in the centre of this enchanting island with its gaily coloured houses, picturesque canals and everything that the artist (and the tourist) craves. There is no sightseeing to be done; we can buy lace anywhere we want to if we want to; we can see the whole thing in twenty minutes and then go round and see it all again. If it is lunch-time, there are several trattorias to choose from.

From Burano to Torcello is only five minutes by boat and on arrival we are greeted by offers to take us down the tiny canal by gondola. We naturally walk and in ten minutes or less are at the unpretentious but luxurious Locanda Cipriani. Just past it is the Piazza and there we can see all there is to be seen in Torcello, which is a marble chair, two little palaces, the church of Santa Fosca – and the cathedral.

Torcello and Venice, mother and daughter, said Ruskin, and we are beholding the mother. It was here that the refugees came first, long before the island of Rialto was inhabited, and the city they built lasted a thousand years. When Barbari drew his view of Venice there were twenty thousand people living here. By the time Ruskin came to make his exhaustive study of the cathedral it had become a spot for romantic picnics and there are in many family albums photographs of Victorians indulging in what James Morris describes as 'a positive ecstasy of melancholia'. Even Ruskin relaxed while picnicking at Torcello. In *Effie in Venice* his wife describes their meal of 'cold fowls, Parmesan cheese, beef, cakes, Muscat & Champagne wines . . .' after which Ruskin and another member of the party ran races round the old buildings 'to show us that the Champagne had not gone into their heads'. They say it was malaria that destroyed Torcello, that and the silting-up of her canals. From the top of the campanile, if you are allowed up, there is an unsurpassed view of the lagoon and the immediate surroundings as they have now become.

The cathedral's mosaics are world-famous, another wonderful Madonna at one end and a gigantic representation of the Last Judgment and many other horrors at the other end. If we have brought Ruskin's *Stones* with us we shall be here a long while, otherwise let us go out, walk round the cathedral, see its great stone shutters, glance inside S. Fosca, buy a postcard in the Piazza and proceed to the Locanda Cipriani. It may be dinner-time. The sun may be setting. It may be out of season and the time when all the other tourists have returned to Venice leaving us alone in this delectable little hotel where everything is done with taste, expertise and style. If all the circumstances are propitious, I can promise you the most delightful experience that even Venice has to offer.

Venice for Children's Pleasure,
and
The Delights of the Brenta

Venice for Children's Pleasure
and
The Delights of the Brenta

I. Children in Venice. I long looked forward to sharing my granddaughter's discovery of the wonders of Venice. When the great day came, we were living in Asolo and so took the train from Castelfranco. At last we left Mestre and began to cross the bridge. I waited for the first cry of ecstasy and, when it failed to come, gently said, 'Look'. She looked and returned to her Dick Francis novel. Never mind, thought I, the journey down the Grand Canal is still to come. She paused in her reading only long enough to board the *vaporetto*. Another pause while we walked from the Accademia Bridge to the Piazza and settled down at Florian's. 'That's St. Mark's,' I observed, 'and this is called the Piazza S. Marco; it was first built . . .' I had reckoned without Dick Francis. Pero Tafur, Santo Brasca, Ruskin, Dickens, James Morris – they were all writing before there was a Dick Francis to distract their readers. We spent the rest of the summer in Asolo without returning to Venice. Where had I gone wrong?

A few years later, when my granddaughter was studying art in Florence, we arranged to meet in Venice. She arrived the day before we did and as soon as we met it was apparent that she had been bowled over as completely as her long line of predecessors. She was hooked for life. I knew then where I had gone wrong.

But some of us cannot wait until our children are able to discover Venice on their own. Perhaps we want to go there ourselves and cannot leave them at home. Perhaps we cannot resist the pleasure of making the introduction ourselves: our children will be different. Perhaps they are, but in case they are not, this chapter is written in the hope of mitigating the disappointment of finding ourselves with a bored child on our hands while we are trying to enjoy the pleasures of Venice. (It may be thought that the whole of this book has been written with a similar intention, but it is easier to find alternatives to a guided tour of the Doge's Palace for grown-ups than for children. Some children might even prefer a guided tour of the Doge's Palace to sitting in a café watching the boats go by, or walking for an hour to find the four Moors by Tintoretto's house; there is no place for dogmatism in a child's guide to Venice.)

There are many disadvantages to growing up in Venice. There is no school bus and your parents cannot take you by car, so you must either walk or compete with the tourists for a place on the *vaporetto*. Once there, the school will be uncomfortable and lacking in playground space. So indeed will probably be your home and

the area round, unless you live, say, in the Castello district where there is at any rate some feeling of space. You cannot keep a proper bicycle, although you can terrify the tourists with your skates; whether or not this is legal, it must be rather fun. There are few cinemas, no science museums or zoos and no sports grounds or swimming pool (although there is talk of one). It is not hard to understand why the unspeakably hideous Mestre seems more desirable in many ways than Venice with all her beauty (particularly since your father can more probably get a well-paid job and comfortable apartment there than in Venice).

Against this there are, and always have been, things going on in the streets and on the water for the diversion of Venetians and their visitors of all ages. Plate 4, for example, shows what looks like a Punch and Judy show on the left, and there is someone in the foreground who, from his clothes, seems to have come from the East and may well be one of many itinerant entertainers. Perhaps there is a hint of what he might get up to in the detail opposite from Canaletto's picture

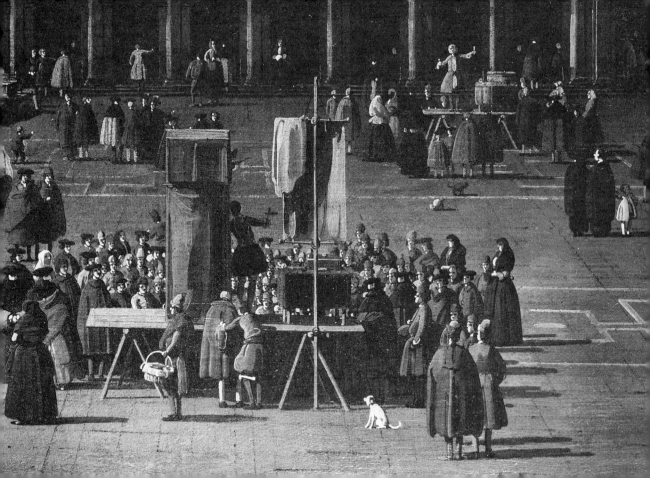

of the Piazzetta where the puppet showman has drawn the crowd away from the dancer on the table in the background. Animals have always been welcomed and Pietro Longhi, whose work we have already seen in several galleries, shows a rhinoceros who caused a great stir at carnival time in 1751. ('Chew Chew, he stands there, plonk on his four flat feet, dreaming of Africa' according to Jan Morris's *A Venetian Bestiary*.)

There are still plenty of surprises if you are there at the right time. If the occasional circus happens to have arrived you may find a fellow tourist such as appears opposite. Since 1975 there has been a revival of the old Carnival in January and children can have the fun of dancing in the streets in masks with complete strangers; even the Venetians discard their somewhat formal attitudes. Towards the end of May there is the 'Vogalonga' in which a couple of thousand boats take part in a regatta for which there are no prizes, very different from the 'Historical Regatta' on the Grand Canal in September which is highly competitive, and looks surprisingly like its predecessor on p. 90.

The Ascension Day ceremonies are not quite what they were in Canaletto's day but everyone does his best, and deliverance from the plague of 1576 is still celebrated, the Mayor taking the part of the Doge. A bridge of boats is still built on the third Sunday in July from the Zattere to the Redentore on the island of Giudecca and you can reach the Zattere by another bridge of boats from the Gritti Hotel to the Salute which is set up on 21 November. You might, in the middle of Lent, come across a scarecrow dressed as an old woman (representing winter) being burnt on a bonfire with children dancing round it, and on 25 April, St. Mark's Day, every man worth his salt should have presented his beloved with a single rose.

But you may be in Venice when none of these events is due and be left to your own devices. There is a hint of what can be done for the children in a letter from the wife of Bernard Berenson, the Renaissance painting expert. Her grandchildren were on a visit to I Tatti, near Florence, which was stuffed with Old Masters which had not been sold to American collectors,

and the three younger children were found marching round the house counting the old 'Madonnas' hanging on the walls. 'They have found 50 on this floor alone,' wrote Mary Berenson, 'and they hope to get up to a hundred. The number of them is more interesting to these youthful minds than the beauty of them.' Naturally. Except for children on the way to becoming artists or, worse, art historians, numbers are bound to be more interesting than beauty. You can play games with numbers and there is enough beauty in the streets of Venice to satisfy the needs of the average child without going inside anywhere. As a start, then, they may care to count the Madonnas they can see while walking those streets before pursuing their quest in the galleries and churches if so minded. Since we are in Venice, not Florence, a winged lion counts the same number of points as a Madonna and a well-head counts double.

There are other games which may, very tentatively of course, be submitted for consideration to children for whom the goings-on of the canals or cafés are not quite enough. The illustrations to this book themselves have possibilities. Where, for example, have the children in the detail opposite p. 215 appeared before in the book? Where exactly was the artist, or photographer, standing for the pictures on pages 24, 39, 43, 44 (a trick question: see p. 45), 46, 73 (point to the window), 75 (solution on p. 76), 98 (again, point to it), 100, 109 (an easy one), 125 (see p. 124), 127, 136 (very easy), 137 (impossible, but try), 141, 185 (solution on p. 184). Finally, the jacket, if the book still has one.

Then there is HUNT THE BELL-TOWER. For this you need the illustrations on pp. 222-3 and, unless you can identify them all from memory, you will have to find the churches they are attached to – or associated with, for they are by no means always attached. The first four will be very familiar and easy. For the following eleven, if I tell you that the first is S. Moisè and the last S. Bartolomeo you should have little difficulty. For the top row on p. 222 you will now hardly need a clue. For the bottom row you may need to board a boat. Be warned that, as well as falling down, bell-towers need repairs that

sometimes change their appearance (see p. 75 for S. Trovaso, for example); these drawings were made a hundred years ago.

The postcards that crowd every stall, and many shops, in Venice naturally vary as much as the tastes of the tourists who buy them, from the Bridge of Sighs to the Piazzale Roma. A good game for children (of all ages) is to buy one or two of those showing unfamiliar scenes and set out to find the place depicted – first without looking at the description on the back but, if this fails, using the description and even the index of this book as a crib.

Of all the postcards sold in Venice, my own favourites are those of the floor of St. Mark's, of which four examples appear above. This marvellous floor is of unfailing interest without turning it into a game, but a piquancy can be added by setting out to find the piece represented. The cards may be bought from the stall at the entrance and, if absolutely necessary, the stall-keeper may be prepared to tell you where to look for the original if he has had a good lunch.

II. Exploring the Waterways. But what is all this talk of alleviating boredom? With highways of water instead of concrete, with boats of every variety taking the place of the bus or family car, how *could* any child be bored in Venice? There is the Grand Canal to be explored, not only up and down, but across by ferry (*traghetto*). There are still seven *traghetti* operating and they provide the cheapest gondola ride available – only half a euro. There is one between the Gritti Hotel and the Salute; one below the Accademia, one below the Rialto, and another above the station bridge. The remaining five link S. Samuele, S. Angelo, S. Beneto, S. Sofia, and S. Marcuola with the Ca' Rezzonico, S. Tomà, S. Silvestro, the fish market (Pescheria), and S. Stae respectively (all these places will be found in the index except S. Stae which is opposite S. Marcuola). As will be seen immediately, Venetians stand in the *traghetti* whereas tourists, if there are any, sit unless they wish to be mistaken for Venetians. Very young children, who will naturally wish to stand, should be persuaded, if necessary bribed, to sit for the benefit of the other passengers.

After the Grand Canal there are the 2, 42 and 52 boat voyages to be taken, and there is still the trip to Chioggia (p. 239) which will satisfy the adventurous instincts of both mariner and explorer. Then there is the trip to Murano, Burano and Torcello (pp. 207-8, 210-211 and p. 241), although Torcello itself is in danger of becoming associated with culture and art-appreciation. Large groups of noisy Italian children, particularly on a summer Sunday, can make the island disagreeable for grown-ups and unendurable for well-behaved English children. And of course there is the Lido.

There is a great deal more to the Lido than the beaches of the Excelsior and Hotel des Bains. There are the *murazzi*, or sea walls, which provide a delightful walk (p. 239) and, at the other end, S. Nicolo (p. 238) and the dunes where Byron rode with Shelley and, later, set off to swim to the far end of the Grand Canal. Thousands of Italians take their children to the Lido to swim in the sea, as is only too evident if you are close to the Danieli hotel on a summer weekend; the tastes of Italian and English children cannot be all that different so it must have something to offer. Most readers of this book are likely to leave Venice without setting foot on the Lido, but those with children should not dismiss it lightly or turn away with dismay at the sight of the buses when landing at S. Maria Elisabetta.

III. The delights of the Brenta. I wish I could unreservedly recommend the trip to Padua on the *Burchiello* for this should be, and for the first half is, one of the most evocative and enjoyable boat trips of all. We imagine ourselves at *villeggiatura* time, the time when anybody who was anybody in Venice went to the mainland and, at any rate during the eighteenth century, those who were hardly anybody at all. In most countries it is the roads leading to the water that become crowded in hot weather. In Venice, where there is anyway seldom a day without a kindly breeze, at the first hint of summer the noblemen for centuries deserted the city in favour of their villas on the Brenta canal. It was not the cool streams and grassy slopes of the country that appealed to them: these were not much farther away than the Brenta, in the foothills of the Alps. But no, they preferred the Palladian palaces of urban elegance which the rich built themselves and the less rich soon imitated in their suburban villas. If it ever was countrified they soon changed it by building formal gardens of clipped yew, marble statuary and interminable straight gravel paths. Once it became fashionable to go, it became unthinkable not to. The only possible reason for not going could be that you could not afford it and, once that rumour gained ground, your credit was gone, your daughter's admirers deserted, and your wife dare not put her face out of doors. Whatever it cost to take a *villeggiatura*, it cost more in the long term to stay at home. Since we are in Venice with our children there is a great temptation to see ourselves as a Venetian family and, if the weather is warm, depart for the Brenta.

We shall not expect to be rowed by our own uniformed gondoliers, to lie on tasselled cushions listening to the music of Vivaldi, Pergolesi and

Cimarosa. We shall embark on 'the common ferry which trades to Venice', as did Shakespeare's Portia, or rather on one of the ferry boats that succeeded it and which bore the name of *burchiello*. They were comfortable enough with, in the words of one passenger, 'a table and two long, leather-covered benches, eight proper windows and two glass doors'. Goldoni called them 'fine boats, with looking-glasses, carving and pictures, that go a mile in twenty minutes and where you can relax, sit down or doze in absolute security.' You will see a *burchiello* in many of Canaletto's works (opposite for example). The Brenta was hardly a *fiume*, or river, by that time. The first diversion of the river to take it into the Lagoon farther south than Venice, and so avoid the continued silting up, took place in 1452; by 1610 most of the river had been diverted into the sea at Chioggia, and the Brenta has become more and more of a canal ever since. To be perfectly accurate we shall embark, if we embark at all, on the *burchiello*'s own successor, a tourist boat of the same name, or its sister craft, called *La Smeralda*. Nor shall we send the servants on ahead with the children, as was the Venetian custom; the children will accompany us and the servants are already preparing our lunch at Mira (or Oriago, according to which day it is).

We assemble just by Harry's Bar, at which we may look wistfully for a moment until we remember the children – and the fact that it is not yet 9.30. Our fellow travellers scarcely seem to be the owners of pleasure palaces on the Brenta; they must either be the servants or, more probably, tourists like ourselves. We move off, following the route along the Giudecca canal which we know from our journey on the *motoscafo* (pp. 201-4) and are soon in the open lagoon with a tiny island ahead of us. It is S. Giorgio in Alga, or S. Zorzi d'alega as it appears in the old Venetian maps, or St. George of the Seaweed, as Ruskin always translated it. In 1859, when he had been to Venice half a dozen times, and his work was at last done, he was writing to a friend about the miseries of scholarship. He had been through so much hard, dry, mechanical toil in Venice that he had quite lost the charm of the place. He was quite sure that people who work

out subjects were disagreeable wretches. 'One only feels as one should when one doesn't know much about the matter' (might he perhaps have had a good word to say for this guide book?). He ended: 'There was only one place in Venice which I never lost the feeling of joy in – at least the pleasure which is better than joy; and that was just half-way between the end of the Giudecca and St. George of the Seaweed, at sunset . . . there is no other spot so beautiful.' He repeated this in effect in his index to *The Stones of Venice* but twenty years later added, 'From the island itself, now, the nearer view is spoiled by loathsome mud-casting and machines. But all is spoiled from what it was. The Campanile, good early Gothic, had its top knocked off to get space for an observatory in the siege' (by the Austrians in 1849). Now, of course, like almost all the islands, it is deserted, desolate and disintegrating. Unless a new Count Cini appears, to do what has been done for S. Giorgio Maggiore, this St. George (who, by the way, is Carpaccio's, or England's) will gradually sink into the Lagoon.

We approach the Brenta now and remember the excitement of our predecessors as they arrived at Fusina on their way to Venice (p. 20). Montaigne, Fynes Moryson, Tom Coryat, John Evelyn, they all wrote about Lizza Fusina, as it was called for centuries, 'where the fresh and salt water would meet and be confounded together were it not kept asunder by a sluice over which the Barkes are lifted up by a certain crane' (Coryat), after which they could rejoin their barge or continue by gondola to Venice.

We must have passed Fusina without noticing it for already we are at our first lock, Moranzani. There appears to be much primitive equipment lying around, yet there is no sign of the expected lock-keeper operating the sluices; everything is done automatically and we rise a few feet only before the gates are opened and we proceed. As yet there is little to see but the detritus of industry from the great refineries of Mestre. Gradually a few houses appear, shabby and mean.

Malcontenta, and we wait until a bridge is swung open for us to pass under; again, it seems to be of great age, but all the man who arrives in his own good time has to do is press a button in response to the call of our hideous hooter. Rather a shock – we are already mooring with a view to doing some sightseeing, but Malcontenta is worth the effort. It is actually being lived in and has recently had three generations of loving owners (the first of these had an ambition to drink tea under an acacia tree he had himself planted and I was his guest at this ceremony when I first visited Malcontenta: self-sown ash and willow have since taken over). The villa was built by Palladio for two of the Foscari family in the 1560's, almost two centuries before it provided the inspiration for such houses as Chiswick Park in London and Mereworth Castle in Kent – just as Roman antiquity had provided the inspiration for Palladio. There is little to see inside the Villa Malcontenta but a great deal to remember, particularly Palladio's genius for making the inside of a really very large house seem as if it would do comfortably for a married couple without children.

We return to our *burchiello* and soon join the main Padua-Venice road (main, that is, until the *autostrada* was built). We realize we are back in the world of the car and how blessed we have been without it while in Venice. Oriago, and another ancient bridge that now opens at the touch of a button switch, followed by another we could get under easily, but no, we must wait until the keeper is found to wind it open. A third bridge, one which the QE2 could surely pass under, then one which needs to be turned by handle intended for a horse, but a five-year-old boy is there to help. What a lesson in the ways of inland navigation this is proving.

A town at last, Mira, and another lock, and there on the left, according to our guide, is the Villa Foscarini. It is boarded up and very gloomy, but we must try to imagine it when Byron took a lease and announced: 'in a few days I go to my Villeggiatura in a Casino near the Brenta.' Once settled, he wrote to his publisher, John Murray, 'from the banks of the Brenta where I have colonized for six months to come,' and a few days later, 'my abode is well enough – with more space than splendour – & not much of that – &

like all Venetian ex-marine habitations too near the road – they seem to think they never can have dust enough to compensate for their long immersion.' He was as puzzled as we all are by the Venetian addiction to the *villeggiatura*. Byron wrote parts of *Childe Harold* and *Don Juan* here, but it was also here that he met 'La Fornarina' (his name for the baker's wife) for whom he discarded Maria Segati, his first true love in Venice. Two years later, on 1 August 1819, he wrote to Murray from Ravenna a six-page account of the meeting and its consequences which reads with the freshness and vigour of a letter written yesterday (Vol. 6, pp. 192-8 of the Murray collected edition, 1976). Soon after that he returned to the Villa Foscarini with his 'last attachment', the Countess Guiccioli.

Now a disappointment. Instead of going through Dolo, which we were looking forward to if only to see the lock which Canaletto made famous by his etchings of it (left and Plate 30: it is still there, although dry), we turn into a new cut from which the vegetation on the banks makes it impossible to see anything. Worse: we must disembark again and cross the road where we wait for other tourists to emerge from the recently restored Baroque Villa Widman which we are to be taken around. No longer can we pretend to be on our *villeggiatura*. Eventually our turn comes and we find ourselves passing through a bar. No one who has reached even the Introduction to this guide will doubt what course we take. While our fellow travellers are being rounded up for their tour we stroll round the garden, glass in hand, and examine the statuary (which somehow doesn't seem to be in the place it was designed for) and look into the stables where there are a few old carriages.

When our colleagues emerge we are all instructed not to return to the boat but to walk down the road to a huge restaurant, where we take our seats under a straw roof. Things are looking up. The lunch, when eventually it comes, is good; the wine, since the Italians who are our neighbours drink hardly anything, is plentiful. The coffee (of course) is perfect. The toilet facilities are scarcely existent. This is almost the best part of the day, indeed the last part of the journey from which any pleasure must be expected. The rest of the voyage to Padua (or rather to its dreary outskirts: no water-borne trip through the city is included) is relentlessly boring. The waters of the Brenta must have sunk over the centuries, or the banks risen; anyway, there is nothing to see. A stop is made at the vast Villa of Stra, for which the fifty minutes allowed to villa lovers will be less than they need; non-villa lovers should note that they are let off on Sundays, when it is closed (but the *burchiello* still stops for the outside to be studied). It was built for the Pisani family and must have satisfied even their vanity and ostentation. Finally we are brought back from the Paduan suburbs by bus. Never has the Piazzale Roma seemed so welcome.

It would be a pity to miss the early stages of this unusual boat ride and the very rich, and determined, might try returning to Venice by taxi or bus after lunch. In high summer, when the car park at Fusina is open, the nostalgic journey between there and Venice may be performed by public transport. Those who take a car to

Venice should certainly go as far as Dolo in it, perhaps on the way home. We came to Venice to get away from cars but, let us face it, they have their uses.

Italian children, although not a high proportion of the passengers, seem to accept docilely the long hours of sitting still: perhaps they are exhausted by gallery- and church-going. Earlier suggestions in this section for the diversion of English children are more likely to bear fruit. They, too, might fail. Do not despair. Remember the second paragraph of this book: Venice is not for everybody. Remember, moreover, that there are many known paths to Venice and perhaps as many waiting to be discovered by pleasure-seeking children themselves.

Solutions Opposite page 215 is a detail from *The Stonemason's Yard* which appears on p. 75.

The first four bell-towers are those of the Salute, S. Giorgio Maggiore, S. Marco ('the Campanile') and the Clock Tower in the Piazza. The following eleven, which are shown in the order in which they are passed on Walk 1 are those of S. Moisè (given in the text as a clue to that fact), S. Maria Zobenigo (what remains of it), S. Vitale, S. Trovaso, the Gesuati, S. Barnaba, S. Margherita, the Frari, S. Giacomo di Rialto, the Apostoli, and S. Bartolomeo. The top row of p. 223 shows, in the order in which they are passed on Walk 2, those of S. Zaccaria, S. Giorgio dei Greci, S. Maria Formosa, the Miracoli, S. Francesco della Vigna, the Gesuiti, and S. Giovanni Crisostomo. The bottom row show S. Sebastiano, Angelo Raffaele and S. Nicolò dei Mendicoli (see p. 204 for these three) and S. Nicolò da Tolentino and Madonna dell'Orto, both prominent on the round Venice boat-trip.

Appendices

The Services provided by ACTV

(Times and route numbers have been repeatedly changed over the last few years, and should always be checked.)

It may seem presumptuous to write in prose about the ACTV timetable. What is there to add to the pellucid yet dramatic words of the timetable itself? Who but a poet, Shakespeare perhaps, John Betjeman at least, could improve on such phrasing as *Servizio accelerato con vaporetti Lido–Canal Grande–Piazzale Roma*? To retire to an island in the Lagoon with this matchless publication would be bliss indeed. It is by no means easy to get hold of a copy, and anyway a summary will be found in *Un Ospite di Venezia* ('A Guest in Venice'), a most useful booklet to be found on the desks of most concierges. But neither that nor the following notes are a substitute for the unabridged version.

The basic service provided by ACTV is No. 1; it is generally No. 1 which is meant by the *vaporetto* (which, needless to say, is not in fact propelled by *vapore* or steam, but by diesel oil). No. 1 runs frequently all day and hourly all night between the Lido and the railway station and Piazzale Roma, taking just under an hour for the trip. The first twenty minutes are spent journeying from the Lido via the Public Gardens (where the Biennale is held) and the Riva degli Schiavoni, to the S. Marco stop which is opposite Harry's Bar. The next thirty-seven minutes are spent on the Grand Canal with fourteen stops en route, for the most part on alternate banks of the Grand Canal.

A glance at our map will show that the path of the Grand Canal is far from the shortest distance between S. Marco and the station and few but tourists would use the *vaporetto* for the whole journey. Those more interested in reaching their destination than in sightseeing will use the No. 2. In the summer it uses the same route as the

No. 1 from the Lido to S. Marco, missing out a couple of stops. After S. Marco it becomes an all-year boat, and proceeds to the Accademia, missing out the *vaporetto*'s two stops on the way. It then, rather surprisingly, crosses the Grand Canal to stop at S. Samuele, which is served regularly only by the No. 2.

At this point, excitingly, the No. 2 used to turn off the Grand Canal at the Ca' Foscari whence it carried on past the fire station (and the remains of that Byzantine house which we saw on p. 97), not stopping until it reached the Piazzale Roma, using the continuation of the Rio Foscari built by Mussolini and called the Rio Nuovo. However, the Rio Nuovo and its traffic light remain *in restauro* and the No. 2 carries on to Piazzale Roma via the station, simply missing out most of the stops of the No. 1 except for S. Tomá, the Rialto and S. Marcuola, the latter for the benefit of those wanting to reach the Winter Casino in the Palazzo Vendramin Calergi. As a result of the absence of stops, No. 2 does the journey between S. Marco and the station in twenty-four minutes instead of thirty-seven.

I have used the name 2 for this service to fix it in the reader's mind but no one in Venice calls it anything but the *diretto*, just as No. 1 is always called the *vaporetto* (though even Venetians may now be confused by the proliferation of numbers). The official names for the two services are, respectively, *servizio diretto con motoscafi* and *servizio accelerato con vaporetti* and it is not for us to criticize the names although we may wonder what No. 1 did before it was accelerated and why the distinction is drawn between the two modes of propulsion since, in fact, they both use the same method, i.e. diesel. Now that ACTV has adopted a single tariff for all services it is no longer vital to be able to tell the difference between them, but for old times' sake I should tell you that the *motoscafo* is almost entirely covered in whereas the *vaporetto* has an 'inside' and an 'outside', the 'outside' having only a metal roof.

The great thing to remember when using the ACTV services is that you are not the first non-Italian-speaking tourist to do so: all you have to do is smile and make enquiring gestures and the officials will put you on the right boat – and, what is more important, going in the right direction. It is less humiliating to do this than to find yourself in the wrong boat and having to pretend that your destination was a different one.

Now to proceed with a study of the more recondite services than the basic Nos. 1 and 2.

No. 3 is the newest service, not in terms of its route – it is essentially the same as the No. 1 – but because it can only be used by holders of the recently introduced iMob pass. You do not have to be Venetian to acquire one of these passes, but it is questionable whether they are economical for the short stay we prefer. On the other hand, you will always be able to use the pass next time you come, and indeed the time after that, and all the while pretending to be a true Venetian on the No. 3.

There used to be other services down the Grand Canal, but all have now been rationalised out. It has not all been loss however, as there are now two lines that perform that most lyrical voyage, a circumnavigation of Venice. What used to be the glorious *Circolare,* or No. 5, to which I have devoted an all-too-short chapter, has now been split up and divided between the clockwise 41 and 51, and their anti-clockwise twins 42 and 52. Now called *Giracittà* rather than *Circolare*, these now logically include the extensions to Murano (41/42) or Lido (51/52). Alas, of all these numbers none now passes through the Arsenal, so that there is no longer any link by water between the Riva degli Schiavoni and the Fondamente Nuove, a journey that has to be made on foot unless one is able to hire a gondola or motor-boat. Those staying on the Zattere, near the station or on the Riva will find stopping places near at hand, but neither the No. 41/42 nor the No. 51/52 stops at the busiest traffic point in the city, S. Marco, so if you are staying near the lower half of the Grand Canal you will have to walk to the S. Zaccaria stop to join them.

Anything would be an anti-climax after the *Circolare*, whatever number it currently bears, and perhaps it was wise of ACTV to scrap both No. 6 and No. 7. The former was in any case just a *motonave*, as opposed to a *motoscafo*, a motor ship, not boat, ferrying between the Bridge of Straw (from which several million photographs of the Bridge of Sighs must have been taken) and the Lido. It has been replaced by the Blu and the Rossa (the Blue and Red lines) but even so we are unlikely to require their services. The rich will take the Danieli motorboat direct to the Excelsior Hotel on the far side of the Lido and plunge straight into their beach and bar life; the poor (and beach-hating rich) will make for the almost deserted and far more attractive S. Nicolo end of the Lido if they wish to explore the island at all. The LN will take them there. The Blu and the Rossa, like all the other boats making for the Lido, merely go to S. Maria Elisabetta which has nothing whatever to offer except a bus which will take you to S. Nicolo and remind you of the world of road transport which awaits you the moment you leave Venice.

No. 8 is a summer service useful only for those idiosyncratic enough to wish to reach the Lido from the Giudecca or the Zattere while avoiding the Rialto almost completely. An accelerated version of this service, the 61 (anticlockwise) and 62 (clockwise), carries on to Piazzale Roma.

No. 11 is now the only means of reaching Chioggia, a journey it performs it in an astonishing way. First you must go to the Lido. From there you take a bus to Alberoni at the end of the island and then change to a ferry boat which crosses the Porto di Malamocco and lands you at S. Maria del Mare on the island of Pellestrina. You then indulge in an interesting drive by bus down the long, thin island for a quarter of an hour and reach the cemetery of Pellestrina. Just when you are wondering what can happen next, the bus stops and your fellow passengers dash for the ferry boat – neither a *vaporetto* nor a *motoscafo*, this time, nor even a *motonave*, but a *motobatello*. If the time is right you could leave them to it and wait for the next *motobatello*, spending the time looking at the Murazzi or sea wall which was built in the last half of the eighteenth century (all of that half: it took forty-two years to build). It is two and a half miles long and has the distinction of being the last great achievement of the Republic. You could walk to S. Pietro in Volta (where there is an excellent fish restaurant called Da Memo) along the top of the Murazzi with the Adriatic on one side and the lagoon on the other, or continue on to Chioggia in time for lunch. There is still another twenty-five minutes of this strange journey before reaching Chioggia.

We now turn to the boats serving the islands in the lagoon – and also that part of the mainland which comes down south to form part of the Porto di Lido and which is called the Litorale del Cavallino. These go from the Fondamente Nuove and we shall use LN to go to Burano and thence to Torcello unless we are rich enough to afford more glamorous transport. The LN only stops at Torcello between the hours of 9 and 11 in the evening; otherwise we must change in Burano and catch the T, which leaves every half hour. (True night owls will also appreciate the direct night service to Torcello offered by the N, or *linea notturna laguna nord*, between 11.56 pm and 2.31 a.m. – but this must be booked at least twenty minutes in advance.)

No. 13 will take us from the Fondamente Nuove to Le Vignole and S. Erasmo, the market garden islands which use the refuse of Venice to make manure for her vegetables.

If we want to visit the mainland we might, instead of Treporti, go to Punta Sabbioni. It is served by the LN running twice an hour from the Victor Emanuel Monument. From there we could even take a bus to Jesolo with its brand new crop of smart hotels and shops, although why anyone should want to do such a thing is a matter of wonderment. We might pause to consider, though, that Jesolo was one of the twelve original communities which elected the first Doge.

The F, formerly the 16, is the boat for Fusina. Lizza Fusina, as it was called for centuries, was where the Brenta joined the lagoon and, since the fresh and salt waters must not mix, travellers from Padua waited at the inn until their barge was hauled into the lagoon or 'took gondola for Venice'. I have always been attracted by the ghosts of Montaigne, Coryat and de Comines, who recorded their pause at what Murray in 1846 called 'a decent inn where they

VENICE FOR PLEASURE

take care of your carriage'. When I first visited
Venice in 1946 this had been replaced by the
Piazzale Roma garage which was already too
small. A modest bribe to the attendant used to
get you in but later the help of the hotel
concierge (the most powerful, but nicest, group
of men in Venice) was needed. Today you have
to be in the equivalent of the Golden Book,
membership of which was confined to certain
families. Your best chance is to curry favour
with a bachelor uncle and hope you will inherit,
not only his 'box', but the means to pay for it.
The ordinary tourist driver will be lucky if he
even gets on to the Tronchetto but if he is
diverted to Fusina he can comfort himself with
the thought that he is one of that illustrious
company who first saw Venice from the Fusina
boat, now the F.

No. 17 is for the use of those people who not
only wish to stay on the Lido but wish to have
their cars there with them – also, of course, for
the residents of the Lido who wish to take their
cars to the mainland on holiday or business.
Twenty times a day it may be seen performing

its improbable task, occasionally continuing on
to Punta Sabbioni to gather or dump more cars
there. No. 18 is a *servizio turistico balneare*, that is
to say for the benefit of bathing tourists travelling between the Fondamente Nuove, Murano
and the Lido.

A more recondite journey was offered by the
No. 19, not currently running. This was another
Lido-bound service for tourists but used also to
call at S. Francesco del Deserto. This is the
island where St. Francis of Assisi landed to avoid
a storm and planted his stick, which grew into
a tree from which the birds sang to him; you can
still see the tree and judge for the authenticity
of the story for yourself. It is still possible to visit
the island, where you are almost sure to be
welcomed by the friars, if you take a gondola or
the smaller *sandolo* from Burano or Torcello.

For visiting Torcello we can take the LN from
the Fondamente Nuove, as we have already seen,
(or indeed from the Pietà, if we are in the mood
for an hour-long cruise across the lagoon). The
best direct way to Torcello is to hire a motor-
boat, at astronomical cost but well worth while

for those who can afford it; you then take your own time on the island. Between these courses, there is a boat operated jointly by the Hotel Danieli and Harry's Bar (with which, of course, the Locanda Cipriani is closely associated) and there is always talk of providing other means of enjoying one of Venice's pleasantest excursions.

No. 20 is the hospital boat which serves S. Lazzaro and the 'islands of sadness', La Grazia, S. Servolo, S. Clemente and Sacca Sessola. No. 20 was used mainly by doctors, nurses and relations of patients in the various hospitals and lunatic asylums which now occupy these islands, but since the foundation of Venice International University on S. Servolo the clientèle is more varied. If we want to visit the island of S. Lazzaro and follow in the footsteps of Lord Byron, we must bear in mind that visitors are not admitted until 3 pm, which means the 3.10 boat from the Victor Emanuel Memorial, and that we shall not get off the island again until an hour and a half later – unless we can persuade the monks to row us to the Lido. Some of us will think getting on for two hours barely enough to

see where Byron studied Armenian, the pen he wrote with, the trees he planted and all the other relics. Some of us will wish there were a boat at, say, four o'clock, but there is none until quarter to five.

The Diretto Murano replaces the 22 and is entirely for the benefit of the Muranesi. What was the No. 23 has usurped the number 5, but this merely travels from S. Zaccaria to Murano ploughing a lonely furrow right round the eastern tip of Venice. If ever there was a service that could use the Arsenal route this is surely it.

Nos. 24 and 25 have also disappeared; indeed the numerate reader will have noticed many other gaps in the numbers, where old friends used to be. No doubt the ACTV directors are devising some enticing replacements. Where will they take us? To some delectable island, unknown except to mariners? To some enchanted spot on the mainland? In the meantime, however, more practical heads at ACTV have worked on modern ticketing arrangements, and on improving the nocturnal services, which now run up and down the Grand Canal every twenty minutes through the night, and join up with admittedly less frequent services to the other islands. And they have created a series of new routes called Alilaguna and identified by colour rather than number – we have already mentioned the Blu and the Rossa, but there are also the Oro and the Arancio. Between them these provide regular connections between all parts of Venice and the airport, sometimes calling also at Murano and the Lido. The journey will not seem hurried; but what better way could there be of arriving in Venice than on a leisurely sail through Murano, around the eastern end of the island and, as anticipation mounts, the inexorable approach of S. Marco?

(POSTSCRIPT. Websites. The timetable can now be found on ACTV's extensive website, www.actv.it, on which the consortium used to refer to itself disarmingly as 'The Firm'.

It is perhaps the only truly evocative website of the many to be found on Venice, which are usefully listed on the Venice Index (www.iuav.unive.it/~juli/venindx). Some of these sites offer reasonably accurate information about opening times and such, for those who prefer their museums to be open. Others have more esoteric material, it might be the perspective view of the internal arrangement of the gondola, or an orienteering guide to the calli and campi of the city.

One site that cannot be overlooked in these pages is www.tin.it/veniva/venetie, which celebrates the quincentenary of de' Barbari's great bird's eye view. Much computer analysis demonstrates, yet again, what a miracle that map is.)

Books about Venice

I. General. It is a quality of Venice that everybody who sets foot there is impelled to share their experience either by writing about or making pictures of the city. The majority respond to this impulse by writing postcards to their friends or taking photographs for themselves and their families. Those who write or take photographs for publication, or who draw or paint pictures for sale, are still in a minority – but only just. There is still room for plenty more. Let us consider the work of this far-from-silent minority. Only its more recent publications will generally be found in bookshops, but the shelves of second-hand booksellers and of libraries will often repay intensive beach-combing.

First the Masters, and first of the Masters, John Ruskin. His works are gathered into thirty-nine uniform large volumes, including the last which is a seven-hundred-page index. In only one of these volumes have I failed to find any reference to Venice. Three of them consist of *The Stones of Venice* and most of a fourth is taken up with *St. Mark's Rest* and Ruskin's *Guide to the Academy* in Venice. I cannot really counsel you to look through all these volumes for their references to Venice (although if you happen to have inherited a set, there are many ways in which you could spend your time more foolishly). *The Stones of Venice* has been abridged by the present author, with many of the best illustrations, and is available from the publisher of this volume. Arnold Whittick has anthologized many extracts in *Ruskin's Venice* (Godwin, 1976) with the intention that it should be used as a guide book – as it well may, but rather as a guide to Ruskin than as a guide to Venice in the strict sense of the word.

Another anthology is Sarah Quill's *Ruskin's Venice: The Stones Revisited* (Lund Humphries, latest edition 2003) but this time illustrated with photographs by the most dedicated recorder of Venice of recent times (her photograph of an elephant is on p. 219). The combination makes this one of the most evocative and most informative books on the city currently available.

Ruskin's wife, Effie, contributed even more to our understanding of the feel of Venice in the days of the Austrian occupation than did her husband, and in *Effie in Venice*, edited by Mary Lutyens (Pallas Athene, 2003), we are regaled with her letters home during the couple's two long stays in 1849-50 and 1851-52. But, with an interest to declare, I must restrain my enthusiasm.

Ruskin and Venice is the title of two separate books which follow this misguided, but endlessly fascinating, man's footsteps. One, by Robert Hewison (Thames and Hudson, 1978), is an exhibition catalogue with an exceptionally good introduction. The other, by Jeanne Clegg (Junction Books, 1981), is both scholarly and readable.

W. D. Howells was American consul in Venice for five years from 1860 and in *Venetian Life* (Houghton, Mifflin, 1870-1907) he, too, draws a picture of the city in the final days of Austrian rule. It has immense charm and was a success when published so that copies may be comparatively easily found today.

Horatio Brown was primarily a historian but his two books *Life on the Lagoons* (1904) and *In and Around Venice* (1905, both Rivington's, London) are full of Venice lore and well worth reading although lacking the atmospheric charm of Howells. Horatio Brown must not be confused with Rawdon Brown, friend of the Ruskins, and another Englishman who found it impossible to leave Venice once he arrived there. Rawdon Brown spent most of his life cataloguing the State Papers in Venice concerning England and, although he published an interesting edition of the despatches of a Venetian Ambassador to London in the sixteenth century, he published nothing about the city of his adoption. He did write a book which sounds full of promise called *The English in Italy in the Fourteenth Century* and Ruskin read it, but unfortunately it never found a publisher. He was a dull writer, as we know from *Effie in Venice*, so it is not surprising, but he was not a dull man.

I suppose E. V. Lucas counts as one of the

Masters now and *A Wanderer in Venice* (Methuen, 1914, and goodness knows how often after that) is the favourite book on Venice of many a reader. It has skill and individuality but the feeling that E. V. Lucas was just as happy writing about London, Paris or Florence is inescapable; W. D. Howells and Horatio Brown (or I) could never have written a series of travel books. They were amateurs, though, and Lucas was a true professional with all the advantages and disadvantages that that implies.

When it comes to those who wrote about Venice in their books as opposed to those who wrote books about Venice, it is hard to know where to draw the line. The index to John Julius Norwich's unsurpassable anthology, *Venice, a Travellers' Companion* (Constable, 1990) seems to include almost everyone you have heard of and many you have not. They all went to Venice, had their say and passed on. What they said is contained in their poems, their letters and their journals and it is all quoted, misquoted and requoted again and again (I am conscious of my own guilt in the matter but at least my quota-

tions are from the original sources and not from other quoters). They started with the pilgrims such as Brother Fabri and Pero Tafur in the fifteenth century, and *The Spring Voyage*, (Murray, 1964) gives an entertaining account of a whole pilgrimage drawn from the journals of a series of travellers: the chapter on their period in Venice is full of interest. In the sixteenth and seventeenth centuries such travellers as Thomas Coryat, Fynes Moryson and James Howell stayed in Venice in the course of their Grand Tours and all recorded their impressions which were curiously alike: in all, though, there are nuggets of gold which reflect a little light on an unaccustomed aspect of Venice. Their work has been pretty thoroughly rifled by now and there cannot be much left to quote (although I cannot recall ever seeing Coryat's fascinating account of the four porphyry figures, quoted on p. 37, and his description of the courtesans of Venice is the last word on the subject).

In the eighteenth and nineteenth centuries these chapters on Venice or references to the city fall thick on the ground: John Evelyn and Samuel

Rogers, Shelley, Wordsworth and (of course) Byron, Thackeray, Dickens and Trollope, Hans Andersen, Mendelssohn and Wagner; one could spend a lifetime digging them all out. None of them had very much new to say but, as Casola complained in 1494 (p. 62), it had all been said before.

Venice has for long lacked a general history written in English for the non-specialist reader. The strength of the Republic was largely dependent on the absence of glamorous leaders, but historians, and their readers, are more attracted to great names than to anonymous deeds. Philip Longworth did much to fill the gap with *The Rise and Fall of Venice* (Constable, 1974) but it was left to John Julius Norwich to produce the first full, general history of Venice in English. In two volumes, *The Rise to Empire* and *The Greatness and the Fall* (Allen Lane, 1977 and 1981) he has achieved the difficult task of breathing life into the Republic itself as opposed to the people who made it what it was.

For particular periods of Venetian history there are: *The Imperial Age of Venice, 1380-1580* by D. S. Chambers (Thames and Hudson, 1970), which reminds us of the days when a book with 130 illustrations, 20 in colour, could be sold for £1.75; and Maurice Rowdon's *The Fall of Venice* (Weidenfeld, 1970). Then there are the books dealing with the cultural life, notably *Renaissance Venice*, edited by J. R. Hale (Faber, 1973) with essays by leading historians of various countries, *Culture and Society in Venice, 1470-1790*, by Oliver Logan (Batsford, 1972), and *Daily Life in Venice in the Time of Casanova* by Maurice Andrieux (Allen and Unwin, 1972); their titles make description superfluous. Peter Lauritzen has combined history and culture in *Venice* (Weidenfeld, 1978), writing as an informed amateur, resident in Venice, rather than a professional art historian.

Almost all these books have bibliographies which will provide abundant material for those wishing to pursue any aspect of the subject further.

II. Guide Books. Let us now consider the guide books, in which I include those which start by denying they are guide books but which are to be read more for the facts they contain than for the opinions they express or the impressions they endeavour to describe.

Some of us would as soon think of going to sleep without a couple of pages of Murray or Baedeker as without brushing our teeth. Such *aficionados* care not whether the guide is about a place they have ever been to or are ever likely to go to. It is the descriptions of travel before or just after the introduction of the steam locomotive that they crave, the advice on inns and on how to treat the native population, details of the post (if any) and of where newspapers may be read and English medicines found. All this is a drug of addiction and addicts have a rich source of supply in any early Murray or Baedeker *Hand-book for Travellers in Northern Italy*. Baedekers are very easy to find but the earlier they are the better: the first English edition was 1870. Murrays are rather more difficult; they started earlier (1842 for Northern Italy) and finished, alas, much earlier than Baedeker which still goes on, but for the benefit of motorists.

They were by no means the first guide books to Italy. The fifteenth-century pilgrims loved to give advice on the journey to other would-be travellers on their return from the Holy Land, and certainly did not minimise the hardships ahead of the reader and so indomitably borne by the writer. Travel for pleasure came later, though, and James Howell's *Instructions for Forreine Travel*, one of the first of its kind, did not appear until 1642. After that there were many, as the seventeenth century was a great one for English travellers to Italy. But none can still be read with the pleasure of an early Murray – almost a substitute for travel as well as a guide to it.

Murray and Baedeker set a standard which has seldom been surpassed. Augustus Hare (Allen, 1888, and many later editions, subsequently Kegan Paul) was so good on Rome but had little to contribute to Venice. In 1907 came Hugh A. Douglas's *Venice on Foot* (Methuen) which has for years been my own bedside book and is the model for this modest undertaking. Major Douglas is more self-effacing than I, though, and withdraws completely on page 7 leaving the reader to walk the streets according to precise instructions with a mass of facts at every step he takes. The book is excessively scarce, although it reached a second edition. If found it must be bought.

In the early years of this century there was a spate of Venice books, often to be found in second-hand bookshops at quite low prices. Such names appear as those of Canon and Mrs Laura Ragg, who leant over backwards to befriend Frederick Rolfe during his most desperate days in Venice and were characteristically rewarded by him by being lampooned in *The Desire and Pursuit of the Whole* (Quartet, 1993) – a novel for Venice lovers, I must confess with reluctance. The Raggs were a Christian couple with far more important virtues than an ability to write with style and Rolfe's behaviour was unpardonable; they must have been a tedious couple though.

The astonishing thing, to me, which these books have in common is the low standard of the writing and the high standard of the water-colour drawings with which they are bounteously illustrated. Such artists as Mortimer Menpes,

and others one has scarcely heard of such as K. Hinchcliff, Reginald Barratt and Trevor Haddon, turned out one drawing after another, all richly redolent of the atmosphere of Venice in a way oil painters of distinction seem incapable of matching. Everyone could paint in water colour in those days, just as everyone can take photographs today. And just as it is hard to take a bad photograph in Venice now, so it seems to have been hard to paint a bad water colour there then.

Those who are attracted by topographical detail must often turn to the standard works on the great Venetians to learn more of the city. For example, only in Molmenti's massive *Vittorio Carpaccio* (Murray, 1907) will you find a minute investigation of the exact site of the scuola for which the St. Ursula series was painted and the way in which they hung there (complete with reconstructed illustrations). Only in the definitive edition of Marco Polo's travels (Sir Henry Yule's: Murray, 1929) will you find a discussion on the spot where his house stood (see p. 152). In both cases, the particular building is lifted from the Barbari view and shown as conclusive evidence. I mention these as examples of the fact that all, or almost all, is grist to the mill of the avid collector of Venetian minutiæ.

Few cities have been as well served in the matter of a truly comprehensive guide as Venice has by Giulio Lorenzetti. His great work was published in Italian in 1926, revised by his widow in 1956 and published in English translation in 1961 as *Venice and its Lagoon* (Edizioni Lint, Trieste). As a bedside book you can pick it up anywhere and just go on (perhaps skipping the contents of the churches) until sleep overcomes you, if it ever does. If it is to be used as a reference book, some study of its rather whimsical indexing system should be undertaken. For instance, if you want to look up the church of S. Giorgio Maggiore you turn to the index of places, not of religious edifices, and in it you find Isole (even in the English translation); under that you find S. Giorgio Maggiore and under that the church of that name which is what you are seeking. The trick is to learn that there are six indexes each divided into many sub-indexes.

Never despair, either, if the page number shown is wrong: the true page will nearly always be found quite near it. Whenever you check a Lorenzetti date the chances are that it will be right, an unusual experience, as every writer knows; house numbers are perhaps less reliable, at any rate in the English edition.

I have already described Hugh Honour's *Companion Guide to Venice* (Collins, 1st edition 1965) as the best guide I know to any city. It is a matchless aid to the understanding of Venice's treasures of art, written with sensitivity and scholarship. Naturally, it is more concerned with the contents of buildings and with the buildings themselves than it is with the pleasure of reaching them – as, indeed, any good and comprehensive guide book should be.

Undeterred by the existence of Lorenzetti and Honour, guides to Venice continue to be published and very good in their way some of them are. No historian knows more about Venetian art than Terisio Pignatti and it is a privilege to be told about things one might otherwise miss in his *Venice*, one of a series published by

Thames and Hudson (1971). Milton Grundy's *Venice: The Anthology Guide* (Giles de la Mare, 6th edition, 2007) does exactly what its subtitle suggests, following the example of Augustus Hare who, perhaps rightly, felt that anything he might have to say on a subject had been said better by somebody else and was worth quoting. As a pure assemblage of useful information, it would be hard to improve on Alta Macadam's *Blue Guide* (Blue Guides, 2001).

· The line between architectural and guide books is sometimes thin; for example, *Art and Architecture in Venice* by Roland Shaw-Kennedy (Sidgwick and Jackson, 1972) was called 'the Venice in Peril Guide'. Since then we have had *The Architectural History of Venice* by Deborah Howard (Yale, revised edition, 2004), particularly well illustrated with photographs by A. F. Kersting and Sarah Quill, an admirable guide for the layman who wants to know more of what he is looking at; the more specialized *Renaissance Architecture in Venice* by Ralph Lieberman (Muller, 1982); and the even more specialized *Venetian Architecture of the Early Renaissance* by John McAn-

drew, a man after Ruskin's heart – an architect who went round the city for years, measuring and discovering things that others had missed.

Jan Morris's work on Venice requires a section to itself. Her *Venice* (Faber, latest edition 2004) has become a classic. It is not a history, but contains much history; not a guide book, but tells of much worth seeing. It is a report on Venice and the Venetians by a reporter – a reporter so brilliant that the book becomes literature. *The Venetian Empire* (Faber, 1980) is, as it is sub-titled, *A Sea Voyage*, in the care of an illuminating courier, and *A Venetian Bestiary* (Thames and Hudson, new edition 2007) is described (we hope falsely) as an 'epilogue'. In between, she has written a perceptive introduction to a sumptuously illustrated abridgement of *The Stones of Venice* (Bellew, 1989).

III. Art and Topography. Reading the foregoing long after it was written, I realize it was no more than a browse among the Venice books I had accumulated over some thirty years. Most of them went as the result of a house move but the new empty shelves soon filled up with what now seem considerably inferior replacements. Or perhaps the appetite for reading the impressions of Venice written by others declines as the mind overflows with one's own. Not so with the pictures and maps of which there can never be a surfeit.

Having started with the Masters of prose, let us turn to the Masters of brush and pen over whom the genius of Canaletto presides. For he had genius, even though there are some who never become familiar enough with his paintings, drawings and etchings to recognize it. Those who want to know all there is to know about his life and to see the whole of his work reproduced on a tiny, but identifiable scale must buy or borrow W. G. Constable's *Canaletto* (Clarendon Press), first published in 1962 which I revised in 1976 and again in 1989. It is a reference rather than a reading book, though, (except for the biography) and few will want to dive into such deep water without a preliminary paddle. The Queen's Canaletto paintings are reproduced in larger size, and discussed with immaculate schol-arship by Sir Michael Levey in his catalogue of *Her Majesty's Later Italian Pictures* of which a new edition was published by Cambridge University Press in 1991. All her drawings, too, (more than half the Canaletto drawings to have survived) are reproduced in K. J. Parker's standard *Canaletto Drawings at Windsor Castle* which was republished, with an Appendix by Charlotte Crawley, by Nuova Alpha Editoriale, Bologna, in 1990. Most of the paintings and drawings feature in the highly informative (and fully illustrated) catalogue of the 1980-81 Canaletto exhibition at the Queen's Gallery, London by Sir Oliver Millar.

In 1982 many of Canaletto's paintings, drawings and etchings returned to Venice for the first time for 250 years for an exhibition at S. Giorgio Maggiore; the catalogue (Neri Pozza) was by Alessandro Bettagno, in Italian. The great Canaletto exhibition at the Metropolitan Museum, New York of 1989-90 showed much of his early work for the first time; the catalogue, by Katherine Baetjer and myself, contains 130 full-page pictures (even the drawings in colour) and essays with much about Venice which will be unfamiliar. This is also true of the catalogue by Frances Vivian for the Consul Smith exhibition at the Queen's Gallery in 1993 and of three more specialized books. *Canaletto's Etchings* by Ruth Bromberg (Sotheby, 1974) supersedes all previous books on the subject. Canaletto. *Una Venezia immaginaria* by Andre Corboz (Electa, 1985) established Canaletto as an imaginative rather than objective artist (no new proposition but treated here in two volumes, with many splendid illustrations). The Dover Press edition of Visentini's engravings of Canaletto's Venice paintings (1974) remains in print. Finally, a new edition of my *Canaletto* (Phaidon) was published in 1994. It is not for me to speak of the text but if you want over 100 colour reproductions of Venice paintings, to say nothing of Canaletto's other work, at a low price, this may be worth looking at.

Second only to Canaletto, and by some as much loved, is Francesco Guardi. The standard work on him by Antonio Morassi (Venice, 1973) has to some extent been superseded by the catalogues of the exhibitions, Guardi (Gorizia, 1987), which dealt with the whole family, Francesco Guardi (Electa, 1993: the exhibition was at S. Giorgio Maggiore, Venice) and Dario Succi's *Francesco Guardi* (Silvana, 1993). The remarkably good value Classici dell' Arte series by Rizzoli included *Guardi* (1974) – and also *Canaletto* (in English, 1970) – but copies are hard to come by.

Marieschi remains a shadowy character despite a spate of books and exhibition catalogues about him, though one book in English on him would surely be welcome. So would one on Carlevaris. Kozakiewicz's 2-volume book on *Bellotto* (Paul Elek, 1972) is impeccable, as to text, illustrations and English translation, but Bellotto, wonderful though his paintings of North Italy, Dresden, Vienna and Warsaw were, was not a painter of Venice in his own right.

As for the Venice view painters generally, there is unlikely to be another exhibition comparable to the *Vedutisti Veneziani del Settecento* of 1967 in the Doge's Palace but the Rijksmuseum in Amsterdam mounted an excellent show of 50 paintings in 1990 with a catalogue called (in the English edition) *Painters of Venice: the story of the Venetian Veduta*. General exhibitions are outside the scope of these notes but those who are fascinated by Venice after the Fall are catered for by the catalogues of three exhibitions – *Venezia nell'eta di Canova* (Alfieri, 1978), *Venezia nell'Ottocento* (Electa, 1983) and *Il Veneto e l'Austria* (Electa, 1989).

But what do we want with all these catalogues like telephone books, telling us more than we want to know, many of them written in a style we find hard to comprehend? The answer is that no one suggests you should read them – unless, of course, you find something gripping when you leaf them through. They are all lavishly illustrated and heavily subsidized by the exhibition sponsors, and they offer us hundreds of pictures of Venice drawn or painted by artists who often saw something that we missed, perhaps because it is no longer there, perhaps because that is what the artist's eye can do.

Some, on the other hand, are for reading and it would be unthinkable to leave the subject of Venetian art without drawing attention to the latest (1994) edition of Sir Michael Levey's *Painting in Eighteenth-Century Venice* (Phaidon) or to his National Gallery booklet, *The Venetian Scene*. *Turner's Venice* by Lindsay Stainton (British Museum, 1985) reminds us that Canaletto had a successor, though not a follower. The view painters were well, if rather meagrely, represented in the *The Glory of Venice* exhibition at the Royal Academy, London, the National Gallery, Washington, and in Venice in 1994-5. Do not drop the catalogue on your foot: the softbound edition weighs 7 lbs. (3 kg.)!

The printed plans and panoramic views of Venice by Juergen Schultz (Leo S. Olschki, Florence, 1970) remains the most useful authority on its subject and is now supplemented by the catalogue of a 1982 exhibition at the Correr Museum, Venezia Piante e Vedute. But books about maps and bird's-eye views are of limited interest To enjoy wandering through the streets and canals of medieval Venice you need a facsimile, or at least a large-scale reproduction of de' Barbari. To know the Venice Canaletto lived in you need

Ughi's plan of 1729. Details from both have often been used in this book and reproductions of both can be found in Venice with diligent search.(Edizioni Tedeschi Marco of Via Fornase 50, 30038 Spinea publish de' Barbari up to full-size.) The only advice I can give is to buy the best reproduction of the de' Barbari that you can find within your means. Ughi may prove more difficult and can be done without.

For infinite delectation at home, Mark Robinson's *Timeless Venice: Discovering today's city in Jacopo de' Barbari's great map* (2003) is an extended exploration on CD-ROM, comparing the map with modern photographs. A weightier tome is *Jacopo de' Barbari: il racconto di una città* by Corrado Balistreri Trincanato and Dario Zanverdiani, (2000) in Italian only, and includes a large scale reproduction of the map.

A plan of the Grand Canal will be useful and can be bought from the stalls or bookshops. A facsimile of Antonio Quadri's description with engravings of every building, first published in 1828, was issued in 1983 and is well worth having if it can be found. Ongania's version of the

1890's was at one time being remaindered on the bookstalls and copies may well be available in second-hand book shops.

The greatest enterprise since de' Barbari in Venice map-making must surely be *An Atlas of Venice* (Commune di Venezia, 1989) consisting of 186 'colour photomaps' which derive from 14 flights across the historic centre at a height of 1,000 metres – low enough for a 1:500 map in which every tree, lamppost and bollard was recorded as well as every human being who was out that day (or at least the top of his head). Everything, it should be noted, except the façades of the buildings, for this is a map, not a bird's-eye view; where slivers of façades appear it is by accident. At first sight Venice appears to be just a jumble of roofs and trees and water but the better you know the city the more fascinating it is to wander along the rooftops and canals, discovering secret gardens and other surprises at every turn. The text is in English, but non-cartographers will find it hard to understand. They should concentrate on the pictures, for this is not a toy but part of a vast map-making project. Opposite every page is an orthodox map of the section but for finding your way around you will be better to rely on Prof. Visceglia's 'Toponomastica' atlas or whatever may have superseded it. Best of all, trust your own sense of direction and find yourself where you may.

Photographs. You and I are not the first visitors to take our cameras with us to Venice. Within six years of the announcement of the invention of photography in 1839 Ruskin was buying daguerreotypes in the Piazza and soon afterwards taking them himself. His collection returned to Venice for an exhibition in 1986 (catalogue by Arsenale editrice) but those wanting old photographs of Venice would be better to go to Osvaldo Bohm's shop near S. Moisè where there are not only books of photographs by Carlo Ponti or Naya but where prints from the original negatives may be found. Those wanting books of modern photographs need no advice from me: the bookshops are full of them. If Venice sinks future generations will at least know what she looked like. Let me end these notes by reminding the reader that in 1494 Pietro Casola considered everything that could be said about Venice had already been said.

The Street Signs of Venice

Although you may often lose yourself in Venice, you will always know, at any rate, the name of the street you are in. You will almost certainly find it commendably clearly shown in black paint against a white plaster background.

Some years ago, at the behest of a municipal councillor with antiquarian interests, it was decided to indulge in the whimsy of using the Venetian dialect for street signs. This is much as if the City Corporation were to paint out 'Cheapside' and substitute 'Chypesyde' in London. Venetians certainly have a marked way of pronouncing their Italian but those who can write at all can generally spell in the same way and use the same words as anyone else. However, it is rather quaint and, to the tourist, quite interesting. Those who wish to carry the subject further may read the plays of Goldoni, who was a great exponent of Venetian, and may buy any one of several dictionaries; for myself, I find ordinary Italian hard enough to master

The street names used in this guide, as a result of all this, generally tally with what you see written up, but they will rarely be the same as you will find on your map. Do not despair: what is meant is generally apparent. Some explanation, though, is necessary of the peculiarly Venetian names for types of street, etc.

A *calle* (pl. *calli*) is a rather long, narrow street but not as narrow as a *callesella*.

A *campo* (*campi*) is a square or open space generally near, and named after, a church. Campo means field and this is what they were one time – with pasturage for the cow, especially in the case of a *campiello delle Erbe* which was entirely for pasturage without even a church. A *campiello*, as one would expect, is a small campo but a *campazzo* is an abandoned place, used for rubbish.

A *corte* is a court and seldom has an exit.

A *fondamenta* (pl. *fondamenta* or *fondamente*) is a paved walk on the banks of a canal. A very important fondamenta may be a *riva*.

Molo is quay.

Piazza is square (but there is only one, that of S. Marco).

Piscina is the site of a lake or pond.

Ponte is bridge.

Punta is point, and the extremities of the city are sometimes called 'Punta di . . .'

A *Ramo* is a little offshoot from a larger street.

Rio (*rii*) is canal, indeed any canal except the Grand Canal and Canareggio Canal in the city itself. The Giudecca Canal and others surround the city; all others within it are *rii*.

A *Rio Terrà* (from *interatto*) is a filled-in canal which has thus become a street.

Riva is *fondamenta*.

A *Ruga* is a street with shops, or at least houses, on both sides, and a *rughetta* is a little one.

A *sacca* is a stretch of water into which two or more canals run.

A *salizzada* or *salizada* is one of the principal streets of a parish; in the thirteenth century the only paved one, and then paved with brick not stone. Stone came only in the second half of the eighteenth century.

A *sottoportico* or *sotoportego* is a small street entered by an arch under a building; it may be covered all the way.

Finally do not worry if you see such words as 'dose', 'ogio', 'anzolo' or 'Lunardo' instead of 'doge', 'olio', 'angelo' or 'Leonardo', or 'de la' or 'de le' when you expect 'della' or 'delle'. Consistency is not a virtue held very high by Venetians, nor, it must be admitted, by the author of this guide.

Food and Drink

In spite of Michelin's generous statement that 'Italy has a cuisine that ranks among the most famous in the world', Venice is no gastronome's paradise. Indeed, one of the deterrents to living in the city is the almost unrelieved monotony of the food. Nevertheless, one has to eat, if only to have somewhere to read one's guide book, so some advice may be helpful.

When Canon Casola was in Venice in 1494 he thought the only explanation could be that the Venetians 'are so occupied with their business that they do not trouble much about what they eat. It is enough to say,' he went on, 'that in that place you could not have a good and fine-looking piece of meat whatever you were willing to pay.' Much the same applies today, five hundred years later.

Veal is the staple meat, generally quite good but dull. Beef is always available but recommended only to enthusiasts. Lamb is seldom seen but to be welcomed when it does arrive. Chicken is the safest bet – and much the cheapest; if you prefer the white meat don't hesitate to order it (*ala* or *petto*) as the Italians, like the French, prefer the leg. The traditional Venetian meat dish is *fegato alla Veneziana*, fried liver and onions. The one meat which is nearly always good is *prosciutto crudo*, raw ham, generally eaten as a starting dish. It usually comes from Parma, and is to be relied on for its quality. The best S. Daniele ham is the best of all but not so reliable. Do not worry: the restaurateur will have decided which to buy the day you are there and he will call it by whichever name you order. It is often served with melon or figs (*con melone* or *con fichi*), and if figs are in season they are delicious, served skinned and ice cold. Quality is rather a matter of luck, depending on which part of the ham they have reached when you order it. Experts are said to have the *muscolato*, or muscly part at the end, kept hidden for them exclusively until their arrival.

Those who like soup are more fortunate. It is nearly always good, especially the vegetable and fish soups – although the *calamari* and *seppie*, which are squids cooked in their own ink, are not to everyone's taste.

Venice, like all northern Italy, is rice, rather than pasta, country and a risotto is the supreme test of a restaurant; few busy kitchens can give it the attention it needs. It is unusual to get bad pasta, except in the very grand hotels where they sometimes try to spoil it by expensive, unsuitable accompaniments. A few restaurants (those of the Cipriani group, for example) take enough pride in their food to make their own pasta – but never, I believe, spaghetti which is said to need a climate only to be found in the Abruzzi region if it is to attain perfection. Nevertheless, you may safely order spaghetti anywhere, other pasta in most places and a risotto in the best.

Venice is famous for its fish which can indeed be good, bearing in mind that the Adriatic is part of the Mediterranean; do not, therefore, expect the fine cold-water fish that Northerners take for granted. The only safe sauce to order is mayonnaise. In the case of lobster or scampi this does not matter, but they are both very expensive even in the most modest places, so be warned. The scampi, generally described as *scampi giganti*, have little relation to the creature which has swept the menus of England of recent years. They are often served in their shells and can be delicious. Sole is moderately good, although also expensive. San Piero, which we call John Dory, and *coda di rospo*, literally toad's tail but in fact a terrifying-looking fish I have been unable to identify, are two good and inexpensive sea-fish. Those whose courage runs high can have a wonderful time with the shellfish, squids, octopuses and many other devils of the deep used for a *frittura mista*, served with polenta; a restaurant serving this fry-up can be detected by its smell several *calli* away. *Sgombro*, mackerel, and *triglia*, mullet, do not, you may be pleased to know, come from the Venetian canals.

Casola and, a hundred and twenty years later, Coryat were both fascinated by the abundance of fruit and vegetables. 'There were so many boats,' said Casola, 'that it seemed as if all the gardens of the world must be there,' and Coryat was equally impressed in spite of the Venetians having 'neither meadows, nor pastures nor arable land near their city'. 'The most delectable dish for a Sommer fruite of all Christendome' was, he considered, the 'muske Melons'. But beware not to hasten your untimely death: they were 'sweetesowre. Sweete in the palate, but sowre in the stomacke, if not soberly eaten.'

The vegetables are unexciting but reliable, although you will seldom get lettuce in your salad. Instead, you will generally be given *favette*, which we call lamb's tail or lamb's lettuce, and which is much inferior. Artichokes are in abundance, at some seasons only the heart being eaten, and *finocchio*, fennel, is ubiquitous. In the autumn there are massive mushrooms, *funghi*, cooked like steaks and served as a main course.

The cheese, of course, we know well from our local delicatessen. Grated parmesan, *parmigiano*, can be shaken over a vast number of otherwise tasteless dishes. Many consider gorgonzola at its best the king of cheeses. There are many others.

Nor is there any need to comment on Italian ice cream or *caffè espresso*, both of which we know all about. If the espresso coffee is too strong, ask for *'acqua calda'*, hot water, to add to it. Try not to remark audibly on the variation in the price of a cup of coffee at, say, Florian's and a café in a quiet campo patronized mostly by Venetians. We in England are used to paying much the same price for a cup of coffee at the Ritz as in our modest coffee bar. The Italians are not. If you do not want to listen to Florian's music and pay Florian's prices, there are places within a few hundred yards where it will cost a half as much, and others ten minutes walk away where it will cost an eighth. Go to them, rather than grumble at Florian's.

Finally, drink. 'Fine quality wines are also to be had, served in bottles,' says Michelin. Don't believe a word of it; the great Guide is just being kind to foreigners. Bad wine is practically non-existent in Venice but really good wine is even harder to find. It is, therefore, idiotic to drink anything but the *vino di casa*, the house wine, open wine, carafe wine, whatever you may call it.

Ask for *vino bianco* or *vino rosso* according to your taste for white or red and you will always be satisfied, sometimes delighted. In very grand places, where only bottled wines are served, express displeasure and order a Soave. This is the local white wine (from near Verona) and wines-manship can be exercised, and displeasure at the lack of open wine displayed, by looking at the label. If it is bottled by Bolla, frown and say, 'Have you no Bertani?' and vice versa. They are barely distinguishable but you will have made your point. That is all I have to say about wine in Venice.

Campari with soda is an agreeable aperitif, of higher alcoholic content than some expect. Italy is, of course, the home of vermouth and it can be instructive to try out the various kinds on offer. Curiously enough, the late Giuseppe Cipri-ani, founder of Harry's Bar, revealed that no vermouth at all was used for its dry martinis, but dry Italian white wine. English gin and Scotch whisky cost less than at home and not much more than in 'duty-free' shops.

I have said nothing of restaurants, except those passed during our walks. The reason is that, like the food, there are few bad ones and hardly any very good ones. *Ambiance* is everything as the food is much the same everywhere. The Danieli roof can be crowded and the food sometimes undistinguished but the view over the lagoon is unforgettable. At the moment of writing, the Cipriani cuisine is outstandingly the best in Venice. It can be enjoyed at Harry's Dolci on the Giudecca, at Torcello or at the unpretentious little Harry's Bar. The latter serves food down-stairs after the international drinkers thin out or upstairs in greater comfort. You wonder how they cope with the numbers without lowering their standards; the answer is a large, unseen staff and a totally dedicated proprietor. When I last saw Arrigo Cipriani he was in a high state of excitement over a new and better butter supplier – this after running the most successful restaurant in Venice for twenty years or more.

For normal eating, though, the best rule is to stop at whichever restaurant appeals to you most. If you order carefully, and look at the prices, you will seldom be disappointed.

About J. G. Links

'Pre-eminence in utterly disparate fields was masked in J. G. Links by a never-failing modesty and geniality,' *The Times* wrote after he died on 1 October 1997. (He had just finished work on this new edition of *Venice for Pleasure*.) Quite how disparate these fields were was always a matter of surprise, even to Joe's friends. He started life as a furrier, inheriting his father's modest business at the age of 20, together with the task of looking after two younger sisters. He soon made Calman Links a byword for excellence, and he received the Royal Warrant as well as being appointed to the medieval post of Keeper of the Queen's Furs. He was also proud of being a director of the Hudson's Bay Company, the oldest chartered trading company in the world.

The Book of Fur (1956) was a masterly introduction to the subject of his livelihood, but readers of *Venice for Pleasure* will already recognise a familiar sense of amusement. Nor was it his first venture into the world of letters. In the 1930's a friendship with Dennis Wheatley, then an unsuccessful wine merchant who shared a taste for fine German whites, led to their realization of Joe's answer to the problem of detective novels too full of 'stuffing'. 'Why can't we just have the facts and the clues?' he wanted to know. 'Not description of the clues but the real thing – bloodstained matches, bits of hair, real fingerprints, all leading the reader to the solution.' Wheatley had to strongarm his publisher into taking the first *Dossier*; four titles were produced, many hundreds of thousands sold and they were translated into eight languages (though not into German, thanks to the vigilance of Hitler's censors). A later generation compared the *Dossiers* to Duchamp and Dada; the TLS called them 'one of the peaks of intellectual, imaginative and typographical achievement by which Western civilization may be judged' though admittedly that was in a diary column.

In the meantime, Joe had become a regular on the beaches of the South of France and on the Cresta run. He also read a great deal of Ruskin and when in 1945 he married the novelist and historian Mary Lutyens (daughter of the architect) they decided to go to Venice for their honeymoon. It was the start not only of a blissfully happy marriage but also, as readers will have realized, of a life-long love. Joe published *Venice for Pleasure* in 1966; and Mary produced a series of unsurpassed books about the Ruskins and their circle. Venice also led to the consuming passion of Joe's later years, the work of Canaletto. His chance discovery of a hitherto lost painting (over his sister-in-law's fireplace) led to a correspondence with the scholar W. G. Constable, who promptly invited Joe to succeed him as compiler of the catalogue raisonné of Canaletto's works. Joe's tireless work on the catalogue, the further books that he wrote about Canaletto and view painting, and the great exhibition at the Metropolitan that he organized when already in his eighties, were models of art history and did much to re-establish Canaletto in the public eye as a painter of genius.

Joe carried on working until almost the day he died, a couple of months short of his 93rd birthday, 'someone' (as Sir Michael Levey put it) 'infinitely kind, perceptive, generous and life-enhancing.'

ILLUSTRATIONS

COLOUR PLATES

Index

Minor palaces, street, *campi* etc. and ACTV stations are omitted. Places and buildings generally appear under the name of the saint or person after whom they are named. Hotels and restaurants are grouped.

ch = church
pal = palazzo or palace
isl = island

Numbers in italics refer to illustrations.

INDEX

PALLAS GUIDES

LANDSCAPE PEOPLE ART ARCHITECTURE

THE STONES OF VENICE
John Ruskin
Abridged and edited by J. G. Links

The perfect introduction to Ruskin's exhilarating and passionate history of architecture.
For fifty years, *The Stones of Venice* was read by all who went there and thousands who could not:
but sightseers whom the city captivates today seldom have Venice's greatest guidebook
with them. The overwhelming clarity of Ruskin's vision, which would eventually lead
to his mental breakdown, makes him the most stimulating, entertaining, aggravating
and enlightening companion. At its best his prose has a precision and nobility
that rank him with the greatest masters of the language.

'One of the greatest teachers – of anything – of all time'
J. G. Links, from the Introduction
A meticulous edition *Jan Morris*

ISBN 1 873429 35 5 £12.99

PALLAS GUIDES

LANDSCAPE PEOPLE ART ARCHITECTURE

EFFIE IN VENICE
Mrs. John Ruskin's letters home, 1849-52
Edited by Mary Lutyens

Even if these letters had not the special interest of being from John Ruskin's wife, they would be absorbing in their picture of the social life that dominated Venice at this particular period   *Marghanita Laski*, in *The Observer*

A lively picture of the *ancien régime* re-establishing itself for its last fling. Mary Lutyens has put so much into the narrative linking these hitherto unpublished letters and is so at home with the vast cast of characters that the book is as much hers as Effie's.
It is perhaps the most radiant episode in Ruskin's life
The Times

A treasure trove *The Daily Telegraph*

ISBN 1 873429 33 9 £14.99

PALLAS GUIDES

LANDSCAPE PEOPLE ART ARCHITECTURE

THE WORLDS OF JOHN RUSKIN

Kevin Jackson

The first fully illustrated biography of Ruskin – with many images from Venice, including
the fascinating notebooks used for research towards *The Stones of Venice*

Brlliantly introduces Ruskin to the general reader and offers insights
into his continuing relevance   *Art Quarterly*

Jackson's pacy text is a masterly compression of an extraordinary life, offering at every juncture some apt
historical context... among the 165 full-colour images are many outstanding and little-known masterpieces
of the kind that only Ruskin's keen eye could produce.   *Art Newspaper*

ISBN 978 1 84368 044 4   160 pages, 165 colour illustrations   £14.95

PALLAS GUIDES

LANDSCAPE PEOPLE ART ARCHITECTURE

Uniform with this volume:

MADRID FOR PLEASURE

Michael Jacobs

The ideal companion we all dream of *Irish Independent*

He has a gift for finding exotic corners in a familiar city and of resuscitating
the forgotten with colourful intensity *Paul Preston, TLS*

Learned but very funny *Daily Telegraph*

Engaging, wonderfully informative and ever-surprising *Jan Morris*

The George Borrow of the High Speed Train era *ABC Madrid*

ISBN I 873429 24 X   £14.99

Forthcoming: AMSTERDAM FOR PLEASURE, SALZBURG FOR PLEASURE

BRUSSELS FOR PLEASURE, FLEMISH CITIES FOR PLEASURE

Published by Pallas Athene,
Garden Flat, 28 Dartmouth Park Road,
London NW5 1SX

ISBN: 978 1 873429 96 9

WWW. PALLASATHENE.CO.UK

*The publisher would like to thank Adam Pallant, Barbara Fyjis-Walker
and Sarah Quill for all their help in preparing this edition
and a special thanks to Peter Khoroche for his work on the index*

*First published 1966
Second revised edition 1973
Third revised edition 1979
Fourth revised, augmented edition 1984
Fifth revised edition 1994, reprinted 1995
Sixth revised edition, augmented and with colour plates 1998
Reprinted with revisions 1999
Seventh revised edition 2000, reprinted 2002, 2004, 2006
Eighth edition 2008
Reprinted 2011*

Printed in China